SHANGHAI IN 12 DISHES

HOW TO EAT LIKE YOU LIVE THERE

redporkpress

CONTENTS

THE DRAGON PHOENIX
RESTAURANT AT THE
FAIRMONT PEACE HOTEL
ON THE BUND

ABOUT SHANGHAI

Shanghai is China's largest city, with a population of 23 million, give or take. Also China's financial hub, it's sophisticated, modern, wealthy and cosmopolitan. Until the mid-to-late 19th century, Shanghai was a small fishing centre, burgeoning only after it became a treaty port in the wash-up of the first Opium War. By 1936, it was one of the world's biggest cities, and was pretty much controlled by a minority population of foreigners who lived in designated areas called Concessions. The colonial edifices that still line The Bund in downtown Shanghai, and the Art Deco – and other interesting bits – of architecture dotted about, are their greatest enduring legacy.

This book focuses on parts of the city you're most likely to spend time in: **The Bund and Huangpu,** for example, named after the river that's such a compelling highway of shipping activity. In this precinct is Nanjing East Road, a major shopping and general sightseeing hub, the main part of which is pedestrianised. Around here are plenty of eateries, from humble canteens to chic fine diners with views. At the western end of Nanjing East Road is People's Square, busy with hotels, museums, a park and access to Huanghe Road, along which restaurants are concentrated.

The Former French Concession is home to the shopping precincts of Xintiandi and Tianzifang and undoubtedly ▷

where you'll end up spending a lot of time; iconic tree-lined streets, beautiful old mansions and a healthy sprinkling of bars, boutiques and cafés make it compelling. **Nanjing West Road** cuts a swathe through **Jing'an,** awash in glitzy malls and five-star hotels; the area is where you'll find the modern art precinct called **M50** and the **Jade Buddha** and **Jing'an Temples,** both of which are well worth visiting.

We've not delved too deeply into **Hongkou** (although the area is interesting) or **Pudong**. But with time on your hands you could easily strike into these, and other parts of the city. Shanghai is generally safe and the worst that can happen, if you get off any beaten tracks, is you'll get a bit lost.

Moving around Shanghai is easy: the **Metro is user-friendly** and very cheap. Taxis are affordable and plentiful, but you should always have your destination written in Chinese for your driver, unless you speak Mandarin. English is becoming more common but mainly among younger professionals; taxi drivers won't understand much of it so it pays to be prepared before heading out for the day.

Unlike Beijing, Shanghai doesn't have blockbuster tourist sights. But it does have a special "*luft*" (atmosphere) that makes it **a fantastic place to simply be.** It's excellent at any time of the year, but note that summer months (June to September) can be unbearably hot and humid, while winter (December to February) is damp and cold. Shoulder seasons (April-May and September-October), when temperatures are milder, are by far the best times to visit. ✱

THE ORIENTAL PEARL
TV TOWER, SHANGHAI'S
QUIRKY LANDMARK

ABOUT SHANGHAI FOOD

Shanghai has a mongrel cuisine, a mash up of greatest-hit flavours from the neighbouring regions of Jiangsu and Zhejiang generally, and the nearby cities of Suzhou, Wuxi, Yangzhou, Ningbo and Hangzhou specifically. There are two strands to Shanghainese cooking: *běn bāng cài* (本帮菜) or "homestyle" cooking, and *hǎipài cài* (海派菜), which literally means "Shanghai style" cuisine or, in this context, **"all embracing"** – speaking to the inclusive, open character of the Shanghainese when it comes to absorbing influences from around the region and beyond. Many of these influences arrived via the legions of migrant Chinese workers coming to try their luck in the big city. They brought elements of their own cuisines with them and these have, over the years, insinuated their way into Shanghainese cooking. The two threads intersect and overlap, sharing much in common – not least of all the gob-smacking local produce.

The areas around Shanghai are agriculturally and aquatically rich, encompassing coastal swathes, the Yangtze river and its vast delta, as well as big lakes and mountains. Fish and crustaceans are important, particularly the seasonal delicacy, hairy crab (see page 78). Fish like carp, yellow croaker and eel are so loved they've been farmed here for centuries. From these varied environs come China's finest soy sauces, vinegars and rice wines, in particular the celebrated yellow wine from nearby Shaoxing and the black rice vinegar from Zhenjiang, formerly Chinkiang. They form the framework of flavour on which much of Shanghainese cooking rests. A complex array of seasonal vegetables is a hallmark; pork and chicken are the favoured proteins, along with fish. Tofu features as does wheat gluten, an ancient vegetarian foodstuff. Compared with other Chinese cuisines, Shanghainese food is known for being sweet, which even other Chinese find hard to reconcile. The delicious sweetness can quickly become addictive, however. ▷

Both schools of cooking share a wide variety of techniques, such as steaming, braising, stir-frying, deep-frying, boiling, marinating and roasting. Techniques emphasise freshness and enhance the flavours of key ingredients; on the whole, mild flavours are preferred. Shanghainese is not a spicy cuisine. Rice is the main grain that's consumed but wheat-based noodles, dumplings, buns and a whole suite of other wheat-flour based snacks (see pages 12, 18, 32 and 42) are much in evidence too.

Shanghai has always had an open attitude to new ideas, both local and from overseas. You find sophisticated food from all over China and beyond – chilli-heavy Sichuan and Hunan food, for example, is popular, as is the exotic fare from far-flung Yunnan province in China's south-west. The Western food served in upmarket restaurants, cafés and neighbourhood eateries rivals that of anywhere in the world and the variety is impressive.

When dining, it's usual to order a selection of appetisers (see page 58) before moving to a selection of main courses. The range of appetisers is vast, including **pickles, salads, "drunken" dishes** (where chicken, prawns or other ingredients are marinated in rice wine) and **fried fish or pork ribs,** finished in a sweet, sticky soy syrup. When ordering mains, select a balance of proteins, vegetables and a range of cooking methods – a deep-fried dish, a stir-fried one, a simmered dish, a steamed dish, etc. For the Chinese, dining is as much an exploration of form, colour and aroma as it is of flavour. The textural characteristics of foods are appreciated – including slippery, stretchy and soft – and some of these qualities can seem foreign to the western palate. A big meal generally ends with slices of fresh fruit, although you'll notice plenty of local cakes around town, mainly made from sticky (glutinous) rice or its flour (see page 118). These sweets are eaten as snacks; dessert, as such, is traditionally unknown.

Shanghai people dine early – most restaurants serve lunch from 11am to 2pm and dinner from 5pm to around 9pm. People don't linger over meals either. Popular restaurants require a reservation (get your hotel to do this) and note that tipping is not customary in China. Many places have pictorial menus which feature English translations – although not all do. Informal canteens, for example, or very local eateries, will have no English whatsoever, so you do need to be brave in these circumstances. Just grab a waiter and point to what looks good on your fellow diner's tables – no one will mind a bit. ✳

Chewy yeasty dough, crunchy crispy crust, spurting juices and a fair amount of lard all intersect in *shēng jiān bāo*, creating the most delicious-est damned dumpling/bun (*bāo* means "bun") you'll ever wrap your pork-loving lips around.

PAN-FRIED BUNS
SHĒNG JIĀN BĀO 生煎包

Wildly popular for breakfast, and easily found all over town, *shēng jiān bāo* – SJB for short – are ordered by the *tael*, a traditional unit of four. And four per person isn't a bad way to go, although the truly ravenous might consider eight and the downright hog, twelve.

SJB are cooked in large, heavy-based pans, often measuring more than a metre in diameter and plonked near the pavement, for convenient takeaway. Generally, the buns are sizzled seam-side down so their tops stay smooth while their bums turn crusty and brown. During the cooking process, water is added to the pan to create steam, the pan is covered with a heavy wooden lid and the buns steam-fry; when done, the tops are pillowy-fluffy and the stuffing – globs of pork mince and some gelatinised stock – is magically transformed into chewy nuggets of sweet meat and a slurp's worth of delicious, savoury stock. ▷

上海欢迎您

Welcome To Shanghai

小杨生煎
YANG'S DUMPLING

Dahuchun, Yunnan South Road

Yang's Fried Dumplings

The fresher out of the pan they are, the better. The last thing you want in a SJB is a soggy bottom

15

Packed closely in the pan for cooking, during which time they expand a bit, the buns end up a sort of square shape. In theory, you could fit one in your mouth in a single bite, but read on to find out why you really, really shouldn't.

Strewn with black sesame seeds and green onion, they're eaten with black Chinkiang vinegar for dipping, shards of ginger for cutting the grease and a bowl of clear soup; the fresher out of the pan they are, the better. The last thing you want in a SJB is a soggy bottom as it's that magical combo of crisp base, succulent innards and toothsome, doughy exterior that make them The Parcels of Ultimate Joy that they honestly are.

Proceed with caution when wolfing these down. That porky stock inside a freshly-cooked *shēng jiān bāo* is capable of inflicting thermo-nuclear damage to tender facial parts... and it does tend to squirt. You have been warned. *

WHERE TO EAT

FENG YU
(上海丰裕生煎 南昌店)
41 Ruijin No 2 Road, Huangpu
黄浦区 瑞金二路41号
6am–8.30pm daily.
A one-stop shop for all imaginable Shanghai snacks, but the SJB are particularly good. It has a very local vibe, with no English at all.

YANG'S FRIED DUMPLINGS
(上海小杨生煎)
97 Huanghe Road, Huangpu
黄浦区 黄河路97号
10am–10pm daily.
There are a few outlets of this venerable store – apart from pork, check out the spicy prawn and vegetarian SJBs.

DAHUCHUN (大壶春)
71 Yunnan South Road, Huangpu
黄浦区 云南南路71号
8am–8pm daily.
Around since the 1950s, this eatery fries its legendary dumplings pleat side up, unlike most everyone else in town. Locals like to eat theirs with a side of beef curry soup (咖喱牛肉汤).

ZHENGYIFENG (正宜丰)
137 Tianping Road, Xuhui
徐汇区 天平路137号
11am–2pm, 5–9pm daily.
With their thick, flaky bases, particularly juicy interiors and filling made from pork and prawn, this restaurant's SJB are hailed by many as the town's best.

COUNT TO 10

You order ***shēng jiān bāo*** by the *tael*, a traditional unit of four. If your *pǔtōnghuà* (Mandarin) isn't up to much, at least be ready with the appropriate Chinese number gesture when you order, so your arithmetical intentions are crystal clear. Hungry local punters don't muck around and they sure don't want to be stuck behind a reticent *lǎowài* (foreigner) in the breakfast queue.

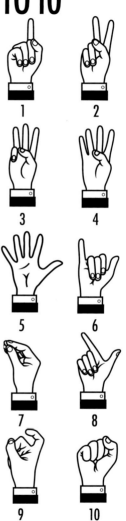

1   2
3   4
5   6
7   8
9   10

SOUP DUMPLINGS AND EGG
SOUP (蛋花汤) AT NANXIANG
MANTOU DIAN

Meet *xiǎo lóng bāo*, pronounced "shaow long bow", where "bow" rhymes with "cow". (Take another linguistic note: "x" in Chinese is said as "sh", not "eks".) The name comes from *"xiǎo lóng"*, the small bamboo steamer baskets used to cook them.

SOUP DUMPLINGS
XIǍO LÓNG BĀO 小笼包

Originating in nearby Nanxiang, distinctively dainty *xiǎo lóng bāo* are filled with minced pork seasoned with sugar, Shaoxing wine, ginger, green onion and often, yes, MSG. The addition of crab meat or crab roe is common; to order straight pork XLB, ask for *zhūròu* (猪肉), and for pork and crab, *xièfěn* (蟹粉).

The measure of a good XLB is in the thinness of the wrapping, which is gathered into a series of neat pleats around the fresh, meaty filling. A good jellied stock, which melts to form a lush mouthful of soup as the dumplings steam, is essential. Better places have top-secret stock recipes.

A marvel of culinary engineering, there's just enough tensile strength in the XLB wrapper to contain the volume of hot matter that forms inside; it's a delicate line between bulging and bursting. Really, the wrapper is only there to convey the soupy, meaty innards to your mouth. ▷

Jia Jia Tang Bao, Huangpu

> **You order them, we stuff them, we steam them, you eat them**
>
> LIN LONG FAN

De Xing Guan, Huangpu

Loushi Tang Bao Guan, Xuhui

Nanxiang Mantou Dian, Huangpu

SOUP DUMPLINGS 小笼包

Order XLB by the basket (*lóng* 笼) and eat them dipped in black vinegar and draped with fine shards of ginger. To avoid spilling the juices, transfer each *bāo* to a ceramic spoon using chopsticks, grabbing it by its top knot, the strongest part. Holding it with chopsticks and keeping it poised over the spoon, take a small bite, allowing the juices to spill into the spoon. Slurp this before scoffing the rest, chop-sticking a few bits of ginger over as you go.

To order, you generally pay a cashier first, take your stub and find a table. Roaming waitresses note your order before delivering hot dumplings fresh from the steamer. At busier places you can wait 30 minutes to eat, so be patient. If you want sliced ginger (*jiāng sī* 姜丝) you'll need to order it separately. ✳

WHERE TO EAT

JIA JIA TANG BAO (佳家汤包)
90 Huanghe Road, Huangpu
黄浦区 黄河路90号 近北京路
6.30am–8pm daily.
Short on ambience, long on queues, this is one of Shanghai's premier XLB joints. Don't be fooled by the simple appearance: outstanding dumplings are made fresh to order by busy teams of deft cooks.

LIN LONG FAN
(麟笼坊特色小笼包)
10 Jianguo East Road, Huangpu
黄浦区 建国东路10号
6.30am–8.30pm daily.
"You order them, we stuff them, we steam them, you eat them" ("现点, 现包, 现蒸, 现吃") is the motto of this sister restaurant to Jia Jia Tang Bao (above). It's tiny like its sibling establishment, seating maybe 25, but is a touch quieter.

FU CHUN (富春)
650 Yuyuan Road, Jing'an
静安区 愚园路650号
6am–12am daily.
Open since 1959, the XLB here are the stuff of legend, with Shanghai food critic Shen Hongfei claiming them the closest thing to authentic *xiǎo lóng bāo* in town. This neighbourhood has plenty of original character.

LOUSHI TANG BAO GUAN
(陋室汤包馆)
601 Nanchang Road, Xuhui
徐汇区 南昌路601号
6.30am–8pm daily.
With just six ever-turning tables, the functional decor (the name means The Humble Room) and no-frills service at this restaurant

belie the gorgeous, thin-skinned voluptuousness of its XLB. Nanchang Road is one of the Former French Concessions' loveliest streets, so make time to explore it after your dumplings.

NANXIANG MANTOU DIAN (南翔馒头店)
**85 Yuyuan Road, Huangpu
黄浦区 豫园路85号
8.30am–9pm daily.**
More than 100 years old and in the thick of touristy Yuyuan bazaar, early mornings are the optimum time to visit before the crowds get crazy. The third-floor dining room offers 14 different fillings and 11 other types of snacks; the second floor has basic pork and pork and crab XLB.

100 CENTURY AVENUE RESTAURANT
**Park Hyatt Shanghai, Shanghai World Financial Centre, 92F, 100 Century Avenue, Pudong
浦东区 上海环球金融中心
79-93楼世纪大道100号
6am–2.30pm daily.**
At this luxe, five-star option, watch chefs make dumplings behind a big window, then sit and gaze over Pudong from a height of 92 floors until your XLB arrive. Not a destination for sufferers of vertigo.

DE XING GUAN (德兴馆)
471 Guangdong Road, Huangpu 黄浦区 广东路471 号, 6.30am–9.30pm, daily
Noodles bring the crowds to the downstairs canteen but the XLB are particularly sweet, rich and juicy, with their thicker Shanghai-style wrapping (true XLB are thinner). This place has a history stretching back to the Qing dynasty.

TĀNG BĀO (汤包)
... a soup dumpling on steroids

The *tāng bāo* is a relative of XLB. The thick exterior is made from a leavened dough, and it's wrapped around a glob of gelatinised pork stock that forms hot soup when steamed. Cooked and served in its own basket, you use a jumbo straw to drink the liquid and then your fingers to tear up the dough and eat that. Fine pieces of crab or crab roe are sometimes added to the filling. Found throughout the city, *tāng bāo* are hugely popular. Try one at Nanxiang Mantou Dian (see **Where To Eat**), where the seven-hour slow-cooked stock is made from pork ribs and chicken bones, and crab and dried scallops are included in the filling.

a tale of
2 TEA HOUSES

There's no doubt that tea is one of China's most important gifts to the world. And the teahouse, a place to snatch some precious moments of contemplative solitude or gossip all day with friends, has long been a vital part of Chinese culture. There are more than 3000 teahouses in Shanghai but, arguably, you only need to know about two.

HUXINTING TEAHOUSE WITH ITS NINE-TURNING BRIDGE

OOLONG TEA AND
TOFU SNACK AT
HUXINTING TEAHOUSE

LONGJĪNG, OR "DRAGON
WELL" TEA, AT SONG FANG
MAISON DE THÉ

HUXINTING TEAHOUSE sits above a pond at Yuyuan Bazaar, accessed by a poetically named Nine-Turning Bridge. It's believed to be the oldest teahouse in China and, as one of Shanghai's most significant historic buildings, it's under constant tourist inundation. Dating from 1784, it wasn't converted to a teahouse until 1855 and, constructed without use of a single metal nail, its wooden tables and stools exude the graceful lines of the Qing dynasty era (1644-1911). Traditional lanterns, wood-carved details on doors and windows, as well as ancient inscribed stones arranged by the stairway, add to the time-warped atmosphere.

Florence Samson, Song Fang

It's a great place to soak up local atmosphere, particularly on Monday afternoons when a traditional woodwind ensemble plays music on the second floor, harking to a time when teahouses were places of leisure and entertainment. People of all classes would congregate at the teahouse, sharing gossip and news with family and friends; secrets overheard in teahouse conversations have fuelled plot-lines in Chinese literature for centuries.

Song Fang: set in a 1930s laneway house

The best time to visit is early morning, when only locals are around; note that downstairs is a smoking zone. A wide range of well-known teas are on offer, including Hangzhou *lóngjǐng*, Dongting *biluóchūn*, Qimen black tea and Anxi *tiěguānyīn*. Snacks include quail eggs boiled with *tiěguānyīn* tea, squares of salty tofu and sour dried fruits. Huxinting is noted for its experienced servers and tea masters, who can give quick and knowledgeable responses to queries.

Tea collection, Song Fang

At peak times, an English-speaking tea master is in attendance.

By way of contrast, Florence Samson's **SONG FANG MAISON DE THÉ**, in the Former French Concession, is housed in a beautiful stuccoed 1930s laneway house. Surrounded by trees, it's particularly serene, with natural light and a peaceful ambience. The decor makes use of recycled bamboo chairs and some vintage flourishes, such as the collection of old Shanghai biscuit tins and 1950s propaganda prints. Opening it in 2007, Samson always intended that it fuse Chinese tradition with French flair and the results are stylish. She says she loves the charming rituals surrounding tea drinking – the preparation, the beautiful accoutrements and the leisurely conversations over a good cup.

Fluent in Mandarin, she works directly with tea farmers, many from families who have been growing tea for generations. She visits her growers, throughout regional China, at least once a year. All her teas are available for sale to brew at home, although she's adamant customers know how to do this properly. Each tea requires a slightly different brewing time, water temperature and the correct teapot (if it's too large, you dilute the flavour). If you don't abide by the brewing rules, (and they happily advise their clientele) you're wasting your money; indeed, some of her teas cost a bomb. "They're hand-harvested and hand-dried", she explains, "and the processes are laborious." Experiencing tea here, where staff speak some English, is a calming treat after the clamour of Shanghai's streets – and that's exactly the effect Samson seeks to create.

TIANSHAN TEA CITY (天山茶城)
520 Zhongshan West Road, Changning
长宁区中山西路520号
9.30am–8.30pm daily.

Serious tea lovers looking for tea to take home will love this multi-level complex, with around 150 shops selling thousands of types. Most stallholders don't speak English but will happily let you taste their wares – note some specialise in just one variety of tea, such as Pu'er or oolong. On the upper level you'll find tea cups, teapots, tea sets and other wonderful tea-making merch for sale.

Tea and snacks, Huxinting

Upstairs, Huxinting

Flower tea, Huxinting

Vintage tins, Song Fang

Lóngjǐng tea

Tiěguānyīn, Song Fang

HUXINTING TEAHOUSE
(湖心亭茶楼) 257 Yuyuan Road,
Huangpu 黄浦区 豫园路257号
8.30am–9pm daily.

SONG FANG MAISON DE THÉ
(宋芳茶馆) 227 Yongjia Road,
near Shanxi Nan Road, Xuhui
徐汇区 永嘉路227号, 近陕西南路
10am–7pm daily.

The number of Chinese teas is a touch mind-numbing; knowing where to begin is hard. Here's a line-up from Shanghai and beyond, to help in your quest for the ultimate cup.

1. ANJI BAICHA 安吉白茶 (*Ānjí Báichá*/ Anji White Tea) From Anji County in Zhejiang province, this cultivar is a relatively recent discovery. It's called "white" as the leaves are low in chlorophyll; it's technically green tea.

2. WUYI DAHONGPAO 大红袍 (*Wuyi Dàhóng Páo*/ Big Red Robe Tea) Grown in the Wuyi mountains of Fujian province, this heavily oxidised, dark oolong is highly prized and can sell for up to $1 million USD per kilo.

3. JUNSHAN YINZHEN 君山银针 (*Jūnshān Yínzhēn*/ Silver Needle Yellow Tea) Grown on an island in Hunan, this yellow tea was said to be Chairman Mao's favourite. Historically it was a "tribute tea" reserved for the Emperor and other dignitaries.

4. DONGFAN MEIREN 東方美人 (*Dōngfāng Měirén*/ Oriental Beauty) A prestigious oolong from Taiwan, grown without pesticides. Heavily oxidised, unroasted and exhibiting naturally fruity aromas, it has a sweetish liquor with no bitterness.

5. JUHUA CHA 菊花茶 (*Júhuā Chá*/ Chrysanthemum Tea) Made from dried chrysanthemum flowers, it ranges in colour from clear to deep yellow, with a complex, floral aroma. Sometimes sweetened with sugar.

6. MILAN XIANG 蜜蘭香 (*Mì Lánxiāng*/ Honey Orchid Fragrance Tea) A distinctive oolong prized for honey-like qualities and an intense fragrance. The best is from Phoenix Mountain in Guandong province.

7. PU'ER 普洱茶 (*Pǔ'ěr*/ Brick Tea) Fermented and strong-tasting, Pu'er tea from Yunnan province is often aged in compressed bricks. It increases in value over time if the quality is good.

8. MEIGUIHUA 玫瑰花茶 (*Méiguī Huāchá*/ Rose Bud Tea) Made from buds of *Rosa rugosa*, this is drunk for its medicinal qualities; it's high in Vitamin C.

9. LONGJING 龙井茶 (*Lóngjǐng Chá*/ Dragon Well Tea) One of China's most prized teas, this pan-roasted, lightly oxidised, needle-shaped tea is from Hangzhou, a beautiful city near Shanghai.

10. BAIHAO YINZHEN 白毫银针 (*Báiháo Yín Zhēn*/ Silver Needle White Tea) A white tea from Fujian province, this is considered one of China's greatest teas.

11. DIANHONG 滇紅茶 (*Diān hóngchá*/ Yunnan Red Tea) Amber-red in colour with a mellow fragrance and rich, smooth taste, this is a high-end black tea from Yunnan province.

12. TIEGUANYIN 铁观音 (*Tiěguānyīn*/ Iron Goddess of Mercy) Premium oolong from Fujian province, its processing is complex and lengthy. It tastes fresh, crisp and flowery. *

You'll find variants of *jiānbǐng* all over China: it's a favourite breakfast-time snack of this food-crazy nation and it's yours for just a handful of loose RMB. Street vendors start setting up at around 6am, eager to catch the start of the morning work commute.

BREAKFAST PANCAKE
JIĀNBǏNG 煎饼

It's said that *jiānbǐng* originated in Shandong province during the Three Kingdoms period (220–280 AD). Soldiers had lost their woks, so a military strategist made them cook batter on their shields instead.

In the modern version, a large, round griddle replaces the shield. A scoop of thick, sticky batter — made from wheat and mung bean (or millet) flour — is spread over its surface, ultra-thinly, using a special wooden scraper. Next, eggs are cracked on and spread directly over the crepe-like pancake, followed by chopped green onion, coriander and mustard pickles. The pancake is folded in half and spread with a spoonful of gloopy *tiánmiànjiàng* (sweet bean sauce 甜麵醬) and chilli sauce. Finally, a large sheet of crisp, deep-fried wonton, or maybe a *yóutiáo* (fried dough stick 油条), goes on, the whole thing is rolled up, cut in half, put in a bag and *voilà* — breakfast on the run!

BREAKFAST
LIKE A CHAMPION...
A Field Guide

千里香馄饨
馄饨
炒饭
盒饭

Step away from the cereal. Leave. The. Buffet. If you're breakfasting in your hotel, you're doing it wrong.

Arguably, breakfast is Shanghai's best meal of the day. In Chinese it's called "morning meal" (早餐 zǎocān or 早饭 zǎofàn) and, all over town, vendors sell a range of morning snacks – just look for queues and follow your nose. Breakfast snacks are no longer sold right on the street as they once were; these days mobile carts set up just off the pavement. As well as the carts, there are plenty of holes-in-the-wall and canteens, some famous for a specific item. For the older generation, a typical Shanghai-style breakfast means the "four heavenly kings" (sì dà jīngāng 四大金刚), namely dà bing (大饼) or Chinese pancakes, yóutiáo (油条) or deep-fried dough sticks, cī fàntuán (粢饭团) or steamed sticky rice balls, and soy milk. Labour intensive to make and representing a low per-unit return, some traditional breakfast dishes are fast becoming hard to find.

Pot stickers

Deep-fried rice cakes

Stuffing a glutinous rice ball

1. GLUTINOUS RICE BALLS
(cī fàntuán 粢饭团)

A fistful of steamed glutinous rice, wrapped around pork floss, pickled mustard tuber, deep-fried dough stick and sugar. Made to order, a vendor scoops hot steamed rice (white, purple or a mix of both) from a large wooden bucket using gloved hands. Next they cram in the stuffing, working the rice so it encloses everything to form a tight, neat ball.

Glutinous rice ball

Egg pancake

BREAKFAST LIKE A CHAMPION

2. SCALLION OIL PANCAKE
(cōng yóu bǐng 葱油饼)
Oily with lard and studded with chopped green onion, these fried flat breads are at once crisp, tender and doughy. Ten separate steps are involved in creating their flaky layers and they're cooked on a flat griddle in plenty of oil. A beef-filled version, tingly with Sichuan pepper, is called niúròu jiān bāo (牛肉饼).

3. TOFU FLOWER SOUP
(dòufu huā 豆花)
Made by curdling fresh soy milk, this soft, soothing, warm dish is spiked with a tasty dressing made from dried shrimps, pickled radish, seaweed, green onion, soy sauce and chilli oil. It's often eaten with fried dough sticks on the side.

4. POT STICKERS
(guōtiē 鍋貼)
A flat-bottomed dumpling with a wheat-flour wrapper, usually stuffed with seasoned pork, although there are also vegetable versions. They're steamed-fried like shēng jiān bāo – you'll often see them cooked with these. You'll also see variants, but the local ones are sort of horn-shaped.

5. STEAMED STICKY RICE DUMPLINGS
(Shànghǎi shāomài 上海烧卖)
Steamed dumplings made using a wheat-flour wrapper and a glutinous rice filling, spiked with nuggets of pork, maybe some mushrooms, a pea or two and some soy sauce. You'll often find them where bāozi (steamed buns, see page 39) are sold.

Scallion oil pancakes

Tofu flower soup

Fried pancake

Pot stickers

Making tofu flower soup

Shanghaif -style pot stickers

Egg pancakes

Steamed sticky rice dumplings

Steamed bun

Deep-fried

Steamed buns

Soy milk

Fried sesame balls

Fried dough sticks

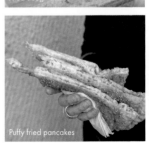
Puffy fried pancakes

Dumplings steaming

Wonton soup

6. STEAMED BUNS
(*bāozi* 包子)

The best kind of portable, doughy breakfast, steamed Shanghai *bāo* (buns) are large and come stuffed with a variety of fillings. Savoury options include pork (plain or slightly spicy), bok choy, leek and egg. Sweet-tooths may prefer sweet red bean paste, custard or sweet sesame paste variants.

7. DEEP-FRIED RICE CAKES
(*cī fàn gāo* 粢饭糕)

A bit like a hash brown in appearance, these simple squares of crunchy, salty, deep-fried glutinous rice are ubiquitous. They're dead-set plain – no stuffing, no sauce, no nothing – and the Shanghainese go crazy for them.

8. PUFFY FRIED PANCAKE
(*qiāng bǐng* 羌饼)

A large, thick, round leavened pancake shallow-fried in tonnes of vegetable oil. Hot, puffy and deep, it's served cut into wedges and is best fresh from the pan. There are stuffed versions filled with eggs and greens too.

9. WONTON SOUP
(*chái pán húntún* 柴爿馄饨)

A Shanghainese breakfast speciality marked by silky smooth wrappers and bright, clear chicken-pork stock – the thin wrappers and deep-flavoured stock set Shanghai-style wonton soup apart. *Jìcài húntūn* (荠菜馄饨) is a version where the wonton wrappers are filled with shepherd's purse, a weed-like green with a mild, herbal flavour.

10. FRIED SESAME BALLS
(*má qiú* 麻球)

These are found all over China and are thought to date back to the Tang Dynasty (618–907AD). The chewy interior is made from a rice flour dough and the inside, which is largely hollow, contains a little glob of sweet red bean paste.

11. SESAME BREAD
(*dà bǐng* 大饼 or *shāobǐng* 烧饼)

Pieces of sticky yeasted dough are cooked on the sides of an upright coal-fuelled oven until crisp and golden. Generally, the rectangular *bǐng* are a bit salty, while the round ones are either sweet or plain. Both are dashed with sesame seeds and/or green onions before going into the oven.

Sesame bread

12. OTHER STUFF

With Shanghai a magnet for workers from all over the country, there are plenty of regional snacks in the breakfast mix too. *Zhōu* (粥), or rice porridge, is popular. Steamed, green onion-flecked buns, called *mántou* (馒头) are everywhere. You'll see imports from places like Wuhan, such as "three delicacies in tofu skin" (*sān xiān dòu pí* 三鲜豆皮), a fried mess of sticky rice, pork, egg, prawn, mushroom and bamboo cooked in tofu skin (or an eggy pancake) and served in small squares. And there's also the aggressively fried *niúròu jiān bāo* (牛肉煎包), from Xinjiang in the far north west. These are jumbo *shēng jiān bāo*, filled with halal beef and dripping with delicious grease.

Steamed *mántou*

Salty egg and pickles for rice porridge

WHERE TO EAT

BAO HOUSE
120A Jinxian Road, near Maoming South Road, Jing'an
静安区 进贤路120A号, 近茂名南路

A fancy bun joint that's calm and clean, with fresh modern decor. The buns brim with a variety of fillings and noodle, wonton and soup dishes are also on the menu.

Three delicacies in tofu

MEIXIN SNACKS
美新点心店
105 Shaanxi North Road, Jing'an
静安区 陕西北路 105号

In biz since 1925, this canteen is famous for noodles and delightfully slippery shepherd's purse wontons. Watch cooks make tāngyuán (汤圆), small glutinous rice flour dumplings filled with sweet sesame paste and served in a light syrup.

BABI MANTOU
267 Jiangxi Middle Road, Huangpu
黄浦区 江西中路 267号

There are outlets of this steamed bun shop all over town; this one is nice and central. The menu runs from meat- and vegetable-based fillings through to sweet red bean and custard.

NINGBO ROAD, HUANGPU 黄浦区 宁波路
The streets around here are full of breakfast places; try Shanxi South, Guanxi North and Sichuan Middle Roads. Just wander. You won't get lost or go hungry.

ZHEJIANG SOUTH ROAD 黄浦区 浙江中路 and YUNNAN SOUTH ROAD 黄浦区 云南南路, HUANGPU
(see Food Streets, page 68) Find breakfast, and plenty of other offerings, on and around these centrally located streets. Food along Zhejiang South Road has a Muslim flavour – expect flat breads, copious lamb and zero pork.

WULUMUQI ROAD, XUHUI
徐汇 区 乌鲁木齐路
There are rich pickings in this Xuhui street, including jiānbing, qiang bing, niúròu jiān bāo and cī fàntuán.

NANYANG ROAD
静安区 南阳路 and
XIKANG ROAD
静安区 西康路,
JING'AN
In an area right behind the Shanghai Centre there's a concentration of breakfast joints, offering everything from jiānbing to shēng jiān bāo and guōtiē.

Zhōu, aka rice porridge

Noodles, noodles, everywhere noodles — the city wakes to the sound of a gazillion slurps and daylight fades to the exact same gustatory chorus. In Shanghai, noodles technically belong to the "small eats" family, although many serves are big enough to stop you in your tummy-filling tracks.

NOODLES
MIÀNTIÁO 面条

The local carbohydrate staple is rice, so it might surprise some to see such a predominance of noodles around town. Made using wheat flour and tending to be slender, handmade noodles are a source of great pride for noodle chefs. Toothsome and springy, they're a textural delight and usually found in casual, utilitarian eateries, designed for a quick refuel rather than any romantic lingering. Some places serve nothing but noodles and enjoy a long and auspicious heritage, named after original owners and earning a cult following for the quality and freshness of their fare. Many of these noodle joints are teeny-tiny and become so packed that, as you eat, queues jostle right behind your occupied chair, waiting for you to finish. For the uninitiated this can be unsettling, but just smile and go with it. "When in Shanghai..." ▷

SLICED EEL NOODLES
(*Shàn sī miàn* 鳝丝面)
FUHAI NOODLE RESTAURANT
福海面馆
332 Xietu Road, Huangpu
黄浦区 斜土路332号

Shanghai is famous for its freshwater eel dishes, including the classic sliced eel noodles from this, one of the most venerable noodle restaurants in town. Local eels are snake-like and, when cooked, present as thin, brown strips with a rich, fishy taste. These top a tangle of fresh noodles and a deep, dark, peppery soup-stock that's absolutely sensational.

CHITTERLING NOODLES
(*Dàcháng miàn* 大肠面)
DAYAN NOODLE RESTAURANT
大眼面馆
105 Luban Road, Huangpu
黄浦区 鲁班路105号

"Chitterling" means "pork stomach bits", and this is definitely one for the offal lover, with flavours that are strong, savoury and unabashedly piggy. A hefty dish, most popular in bitingly cold winter months, the full-bodied soup brims with rich seasoning and soft chunks of pork intestines. Load your bowl with fresh coriander and oily chilli paste, which you throw on to taste.

SESAME PASTE NOODLES
(*Májiàng miàn* 麻酱面)
WEI XIANG ZHAI
味香斋(雁荡路店)
14 Yandang Road, Huangpu
黄浦区 雁荡路14号

It's a daily crush here and people come for just one thing – sesame paste noodles, maybe with a side of beef soup (*niúròu tāng* 小牛汤). A heavenly mixture of fresh noodles, sesame paste, chilli oil and green onion, this is as good as the holy trinity of hot-sweet-salty flavours gets. Table turnover is quick, so hover until a seat becomes free. Order and pay first, wave your coupons at the wait staff and hoe in.

YELLOW CROAKER NOODLES
(*Huángyú miàn* 黄鱼面)
ANIANGMIAN RESTAURANT
阿娘面
36 Sinan Road, Huangpu
黄浦区 思南路36号

Arguably the most famous Shanghai noodle shop, it opens at 11am, when it's stormed by the lunch rush. Come later, at about 5pm, if you prefer a less frenetic vibe. Run by the original vendor's grandson, The Dish to order here is the fish noodle one, made using fillets of yellow croaker, a prized table fish, and featuring a particularly luscious stock.

DUCK LEG NOODLES
(*Yā tuǐ miàn* 鸭腿麵)
YONGXING NOODLE RESTAURANT
永兴面馆
448-454 Guangxi North Road, Huangpu
黄浦区 广西北路 448-454号
Exploring the streets adjoining Nanjing East Road has plenty of rewards. Cheek by jowl with the shopping frenzy is this grungy slice of authentic Shanghai life – a worker's canteen. You'll get a warm welcome and a hot bowl of the best duck leg noodles around. Spicy pork noodles are also very good here.

BULLFROG NOODLES
(*Niúwā miàn* 牛蛙面)
HALING NOODLE RESTAURANT
哈灵面馆
8 Guangxi South Road, Huangpu
黄浦区 广西南路8号
Sturdy, round, chewy noodles swim in a thick, yellow broth studded generously with the soft, white and mild meat of two or three bullfrogs and plenty of green pepper; a huge bowl will set you back around 30RMB. Bullfrog tastes a bit like chicken and is meant to stimulate appetite and "rebalance" your stomach. It's very popular in Shanghai.

PORK LIVER NOODLES
(*Zhū gān miàn* 猪肝面)
**BAOTAI NOODLE
RESTAURANT** 宝泰面馆
No 1, Lane 1072 Quxi Road,
Huangpu
黄浦区 瞿溪路1072弄1号
Small, hidden down an alley and
with a resolutely old-time feel,
Baotai services night-owls in search
of a stomach-lining snack. Opening
at 2pm and closing at 5am, their
recipes haven't changed for
decades. The gutsy pork liver
noodles, topped with copious,
tender slices of this love-or-hate
offal and a rich, meaty stock, is one
of the best versions in town.

PORK CUTLET NOODLES
(*Zhà zhūpái miàn* 炸猪排面)
MEIXIN SNACKS
美新点心店
105 Shaanxi North Road, Jing'an
静安区 陕西北路105号
Open since 1925, this homey,
canteen-style place serves 1000
people a day, so they say. It's
always a toss-up between the
famed cold pork noodles – a mix of
chilli oil, peanut sauce, vinegar and
pork bits over cold noodles – and
the pork cutlet noodles, with the
chop eaten on the side. Or, thrust
right into the soup and devoured in
alternating bites of broth, noodles
and meat. *

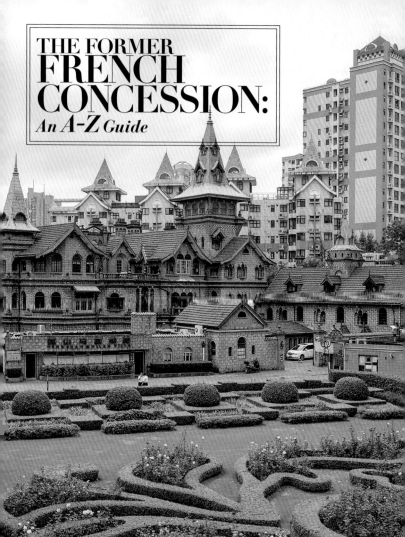

THE FORMER FRENCH CONCESSION:
An A-Z Guide

THE 1930s GOTHIC-TUDOR
MOLLER VILLA HOTEL

Loosely, the old districts of LUWAN AND XUHUI COMPRISE THE FORMER FRENCH CONCESSION, home to swathes of gorgeous old mansions, shady, tree-lined streets, chichi boutiques, cafés, bars and historic bits of landmark architecture. You're going to want to hang out here; it's a breath of fresh air after the relentless crush of downtown Shanghai. Not that its streets are sleepy — far from it.

Designated a Concession area between 1849 and 1943, where foreign law reigned and Chinese access was limited, the FFC has always exuded a distinctly European flavour. Back in the day, it was the premier retail and residential heart of the city and it's still one of THE places to live, shop and drink. Here's an A-to-Z starter pack of its highlights, including bars, eateries, shops and architectural must-sees.

Boutique beers at Boxing Cat Brewery

A NFU ROAD
安福路

One of the FFC's loveliest streets, Anfu Road is dotted with cafés, galleries, boutiques and bars. **Baker + Spice** (No 195) has brilliant coffee, doughnuts, sandwiches and the like. Swoop by **Piling Pelang** (No 183) for gorgeous ceramic and cloisonné homewares inspired by traditional oriental designs.

B OXING CAT BREWERY
82 Fuxing West Road
复兴西路82号

An American-style boutique brewery with outdoor terraces and fantastic, house-brewed beers – a saviour after the ubiquitous commercial offerings around town.

C HANGLE ROAD
长乐路

Quirky local boutiques, a bit of vintage shopping and interesting people watching are to be had along here. "C" is also for the complimentary crisp cookies you get with your tea at **Annvita Tea Room** (Building 27, 519 Fuxing Middle Road, 复兴中路519号27栋).

D AGA BREWPUB
100 Fuxing West Road
复兴西路100号

Specialising in Chinese craft beers from Beijing, Chengdu, Nanjing et al, this pub has beers you won't find elsewhere in town. The rooftop is an excellent place to kick back.

Baker + Spice

Daga Brewpub

Annvita Tea Room

French pastry at Farine

FORMER FRENCH CONCESSION

E CCLESIASTICAL
16 Gaolan Road
皋兰路, 16 号

Get your Orthodox on at St Nicholas Church, evidence of Shanghai's polyglot past. Built by the Russian community in 1934, it was once, post 1949, used as a washing machine factory.

F ARINE
378 Wukang Road
武康路378号1楼

Queues form for arguably the best French-style artisanal baking in Shanghai. The outdoor terrace, facing pretty Wukang Road (more than worthy of a stroll, by the way), is a coveted spot.

G RAINS
202 Wukang Road
武康路202号

A woody, modern space where the excellent coffee (try the iced brew in hot weather) and delicious house-made ice cream, served from a street window, are the G.O.

European-style mansion

HUAIHAI MIDDLE ROAD
淮海中路

One of Shanghai's main shopping streets. Divided into three sections, it's the 5.5km-long middle stretch that's best for swanky, big-brand shopping – you haven't been to Shanghai unless you've hung out here.

Brocade queen Liu Xiaolan

INTERCONTINENTAL SHANGHAI RUIJIN
118 Ruijin No 2 Road
瑞金二路118号

Dating from 1924 and now an opulent hotel, the four original villas and 7ha of gardens were once reserved for dignitaries like Chiang Kai Shek, Nehru, Kim Il Sung, Ho Chi Minh and Nixon.

Brocade Country

JULU ROAD
巨鹿路

Great dining options abound, like the Taiwanese fusion place **People 7** (No 805) and **Lost Heaven** (No 758), for upscale Yunnan food. Shoppers, head to **Brocade Country** (No 616), Liu Xiaolan's boutique specialising in textiles, jewels and clothing from Guizhou.

KAPPO YU
33 Wuxing Road
吴兴路33号

This stellar Japanese diner is tiny, with two private rooms and a counter seating 20. The 10-course seasonal set menu changes with every full moon and the Tokyo-born chef is ex-Nobu.

Yunnan food at Lost Heaven

FORMER FRENCH CONCESSION

LYCEUM AND CATHAY THEATERS

A relic of Shanghai's art deco heyday, the Lyceum (**57 Maoming South Road, 茂名南路57号**) is one of Shanghai's oldest theatres. Built in 1930, it still hosts live performances. The Cathay, (**870 Huaihai Middle Road, 淮海中路870号**), is of similar age and still operates as a movie theatre.

MOLLER VILLA HOTEL
30 Shanxi South Road 陕西南路30号

With its fantastical Gothic-Tudor embellishments, this 1936 villa is now a hotel. It's one of Shanghai's most impressive historic buildings; the original owner was the chair of the Shanghai Race Club and a shipping magnate.

The art deco Cathy Theatre

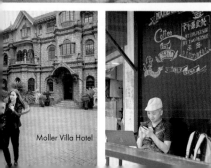

Moller Villa Hotel

NORMANDIE BUILDING
1850 Huaihai Middle Road 淮海中路1850号

Designed by Hungarian architect László Hudec, this 1920s block has been home to many celebrities over the years. "N" is also for the charming **Nanxiang Tea Shop** (18 Fuxing Middle Road 复兴中路18号) purveyors of top-notch Chinese teas and Yixing teapots.

OKURA GARDEN HOTEL
58 Maoming Nan Lu 茂名南路58号

This former French Club still bears vestiges of its grand 1920s past. The ballroom is spectacular, with a sprung dance floor and stained glass ceiling. Check out the second-floor plasterwork nudes.

PROPAGANDA POSTER ART CENTRE
Basement, Bldg B, 868 Huashan Lu, near Zhenning Lu 华山路868号B号楼,近镇宁路

Shining a spotlight on a troubled period of China's recent history, the collection of 1960s -1970s originals here is amazing. For "P" there's also **Project Aegis** (1 Taojiang Road, 桃江路1号) for brilliant coffee and men's clothing; and even a Pushkin monument.

QIPAO
旗袍

Maoming Road is the destination for sexy, tailor-made *qípáo* (cheongsam), some embellished with glorious hand embroidery. Start at the

Normandie Building

Pushkin Monument

Song Qing Ling residence

Statue of Song Qing Ling

Propaganda Poster Art Centre

FORMER FRENCH CONCESSION

amazing **Jin Zhi Yu Ye (72 Maoming South Road 茂名南路 72号, 近淮海中路)** and wander at will from there.

RESIDENCE OF SONG QING LING 上海宋庆龄故居

1843 Huaihai Middle Road 淮海中路1843号

A fascinating glimpse into the life of a major Chinese political and social figure; history buffs will be fascinated. The 1920s house and garden are stunning.

SPEAK LOW
579 Fuxing Middle Road 复兴中路579号

Boasting three bars-within-bars and evoking a 1920s speakeasy, the entrance to the second bar is hidden: press a concealed button on a map of Shanghai to enter. The matcha-based Speak Low cocktail has won global awards.

Cheongsam on Maoming Road

TIANZIFANG
田子坊
210 Taikang Road
泰康路210弄

Fashioned around old laneway houses, this frenzied shopping precinct is an excellent place for souvenirs and gifts, with everything on offer from Tibetan jewellery to fridge magnets and locally-designed children's wear.

URBAN TRIBE
133 Fuxing West Road,
复兴西路133号

Urban Tribe

Beautiful clothes, locally designed in a loose, flowing style made from quality fabrics, is their thing. The statement jewellery pieces, also locally made, are mighty tempting.

VOLCAN
80 Yongkang Road
永康路80号

Rice wine, Yintiandi

Yongkang Road is famous for cafés and bars and it's a beloved expat hangout. Weeny Café del Volcán stands out for excellent coffee; they roast their own beans. Griffin Coffee (No 84) is also pretty darned good.

WULUMUQI ROAD
乌鲁木齐路

A bustling, character-filled street with a compelling mix of local charm and polished European influences. Check out **Kate Wood Originals** (No 336-338) for stylish bamboo sunnies and watches, and the cult-followed **Feiyue** sneaker shop at No 206.

Shopping at Tianzifang

Nanxiang Tea Shop

Hanzifang finds

Zen Lifestore

FORMER FRENCH CONCESSION

X INTIANDI
上海新天地
Lane 181, Taicang Road
太仓路181弄

A precinct of restaurants, cafés bars and shops built around historic homes, Xintiandi is on every visitor's list. Eat, drink, shop and drool over Shanghai Tang's China-esque designer goods.

Y ONGFOO ELITE
200 Yongfu Road
永福路200号

A restaurant in a dazzling property that once housed the Vietnamese Consulate. Packed with antiques, the interiors are dreamy; the food is not cheap but the vibe is so worth it.

Z EN LIFESTORE
7-1 Dongping Road
东平路7-1号近衡山路

The place for pretty porcelain products, inspired by Chinese motifs and icons. Many are hand-painted in Jingdezhen, China's porcelain capital. ✱

57

CENTURY EGGS
(*PÍDÀN* 皮蛋) WITH CHILLI
AND SIMPLE SNACKS

Not so much a single dish as an entire family of them, the appetiser course is a real joy of the Shanghai menu and one you shouldn't miss. It's hard to pick a favourite dish as the repertoire is huge and varied, with plenty of standard menu items boosted through the year by seasonal offerings.

APPETISERS
KĀIWÈI CÀI 开胃菜

You could easily fill up on appetisers in Shanghai and skip main course altogether. Best shared in a group so you can sample more of them, some of these dishes are dainty and light, while others are gutsy and rustic. Many are served cold. Their flavours and textures encompass the full sweep, from rich, oily, sweet, luscious, crisp, fresh and sharp through to smooth, slippery, salty, soft and crunchy.

Vegetables, fish, tofu, meats, fungi, eggs, sprouts, dried beans and legumes are all employed as key ingredients in appetisers. Some appetisers lean toward the exotic: **duck tongues, duck webs, pig ears, chicken feet** and **jellyfish,** for example. Some are dead-set simple and are rustled up just before serving: **boiled peanuts** or **wedges of century egg**, fall into this category. Others are way more complex, requiring elaborate, advance preparation, such as chewy **slices of preserved** ▷

Shanghai Tang Cafe

Pickled radish

Fennel-scented beans

Roast "goose"

Fresh soy beans in rice wine

De Xing Guan

Salted fish

Crispy fish

(salted) fish (鹹魚) or **crystal pork terrine** (水晶肴肉), served in perfect, aspic-topped slices.

There's a whole family of **"drunken" dishes,** where the main ingredient (such as chicken, prawns and crabs) are steeped in Shaoxing wine; **drunken chicken** (醉雞) is maybe the most famous example.

Another famous dish is called **"smoked fish"** (上海熏鱼) which, confusingly, isn't smoked at all. Slices of meaty, white fish are marinated in a dark, sticky, aromatic soy sauce mixture then deep-fried. Served at room temperature, the fish is burnished and chewy on the outside, and soft and yielding within.

Then there's **braised wheat gluten** (紅燒烤麩), a great dish for vegetarians. Chunks of gluten (an ancient Chinese meat substitute made by washing wheat flour dough until only a mass of gluten remains) are braised with "four delights," namely dried lily flowers, wood ear mushrooms, peanuts and shiitake mushrooms, flavoured with soy, ginger, star anise and wine.

Roast "goose" (煙燻素鵝) isn't goose at all, but a sliced affair of tofu skin stuffed with vegetables or mushrooms, then fried until crisp on the outside and chewy inside.

Mashed broad beans (豆瓣酥) are simple and soulful; **pickled radish** (爽口甜辣腌萝卜) is crisp and lively.

Chicken in scallion oil (葱油鸡) is made using a single small yellow-skinned bird, poached whole then served cut through the bone and drenched in an unctuous green onion (scallion)-infused oil. ∗

Many Shanghai appetisers are soy, wine and vinegar infused, but some are all about the sugar. You'd be forgiven for thinking **lotus root with sticky rice** (糯米藕) was a dessert, with its glossy syrup coating and scattering of osmanthus flowers. Served in slices, either warm or at room temperature, it's pretty and delicious.

Then there's **glutinous rice-stuffed red dates** (心太软) (above). Seeded red dates, stuffed with glutinous rice paste, are steamed then steeped in thick, sugary syrup and are even sweeter than their lotus root counterparts. It may seem strange to eat sugary and savoury morsels together, at the start of a meal, but that's exactly what the locals love to do. Just roll with it. Try these dishes at Old Jesse (see pages 85, 111).

Celtuce, celery, pumpkin, mushrooms, lily buds, eggplant and cabbage also star in simple, salad-like dishes. One of the most distinctive of these is **minced green leaf and tofu salad** (香干馬蘭頭), redolent of sesame oil and refreshingly light after the fatty richness of Shanghai's meat dishes. Glossy with soy sauce, sugar, sesame oil and cooking wine, **soy sauce greens** (宁波火靠菜) is an import from nearby Ningbo and demonstrates the local love of sweet and sour flavours. It's derived in this case, as it is in many others, from a combination of soy sauce, sugar and Shaoxing wine. ✳

DRUNKEN CHICKEN
AT XINDALU

Pumpkin with red dates and glutinous rice

De Xing Guan

Drunken prawns

WHERE TO EAT

Most Shanghainese restaurants serve a range of appetisers, so it's hard to single out any in particular. Here are a few picks.

DRAGON PHOENIX (龙凤厅)

8F, Fairmont Peace Hotel, 20 Nanjing East Road, Huangpu
黄浦区 南京东路20号 和平饭店北楼8楼
11am–2.30pm, 5.30–10.30pm daily.
The menu skews towards Cantonese but there are a few local offerings. The vintage dining room, right on the Bund, is spectacular.

JIAN GUO 328 (建国328小馆)

328 Jiangguo West Road, Xuhui
徐汇区 建国西路328 号
11am –9.30pm daily.
A buzzy, famous local eatery that eschews MSG and only uses premium-quality produce. The cold mushroom in soy sauce (卤水大花蘑菇) is excellent.

XINDALU (新大陆中国厨房)

Hyatt On The Bund, 199 Huangpu Road,Hongkou
黄浦路199号上海外滩 茂悦大酒店东楼大堂
11.30am–2.30pm, 5.30–10.30pm daily.
One of the best places to dine in town (see page

89). Presentation is modern and ingredients are top-notch; the menu features more than 30 appetisers. Service, in keeping with a five-star property, is polished.

QIAO FAMILY GATE (乔家栅食府)

336 Xiangyang Road, Xuhui,
徐汇区 襄阳南路336 号
8am–10pm daily.
An unassuming place frequented by locals; the stand-out appetiser here is the cold chicken in scallion oil.

SHANGHAI TANG CAFE (上海滩)

2F-3F, 333 Huangpi South Road, Xintiandi,
黄陂南路333号2-3楼
11am–2.30pm, 5.30–10pm daily.
The decor, drawing on the design aesthetic of the eponymous fashion house, is superb and the location, in Xintiandi, is excellent. The modernised food is a few cuts above too.

DE XING GUAN (上海德兴面馆, 广东路总店)

471 Guangdong Road, Huangpu
黄浦区 广东路471号
11am–2pm, 5–9.30pm daily.
This venerable restaurant, established in 1878, serves 20 types of noodles downstairs, and a roll-call of Shanghainese greats upstairs. The drunken chicken is a winner.

A PLATE OF PORK
WITH RICE CAKES,
LAO SHENG XING

Imagine the greasiest thing you possibly can — foie gras poutine, battered cheese-crust pizza, deep-fried butter. Now eat THIS delectable gut buster: a crisp, deep-fried pork chop, served on thick, chewy rice cakes, the whole thing slathered in a gooey, sweet-salty sauce. Mmmmmmm... It's fair to say the Shanghainese aren't afraid of fat.

PORK WITH RICE CAKES
PÁIGǓ NIÁNGāO 排骨年糕

Pork with rice cakes is a nostalgic favourite, with its family-style flavours and sling-it-on-the-plate presentation. Perhaps the most famous iteration is found on Yunnan South Road's Xian De Lai, established in 1921. It's an old-school place where you order with the cashier, get your meal ticket then wave it at a server. They sell thousands of portions of *páigǔ niángāo* each day and the head chef has been cooking the dish for some 40 years.

Where other places simply fry their pork, here they blanch it first (they use a boneless pork chop), marinate it in aromatics, dust it with flour and five spice and then hurl it in the oil. The exterior isn't crisp, but more soft and chewy and the secret house-recipe sauce is delightfully gloopy. It's not hard to see traces of Western influence in this dish, dating as it does from early last century when large European populations lived in the city — it's unusual for Chinese to cook meat in big bits like this. ▷

PORK WITH RICE CAKES 排骨年糕

Shanghainese *niángāo* are the flat, canoe-shaped glutinous rice cakes the pork rests on; the name means "year cake." They're bland and wonderfully chewy, absorbing sauce like you wouldn't believe. You'll see them in other dishes around town too, such as stir fried *niángāo* (炒年糕), where they're cooked with ingredients like beef or pork, green onion, cabbage, soy and ginger, and add a delightful textural interest. They can also turn up in soups.

Pork preparation, Xian De Lai

> ❝ **Shanghai-style *niángāo* are bland and wonderfully chewy, absorbing sauce like you wouldn't believe** ❞

LÀ JIÀNG YÓU

Là jiàng yóu (辣酱油) is a **unique Shanghai condiment that accompanies** *páigǔ niángāo*; you drizzle it over, to taste. The name translates as **"spicy soy sauce" but it's more like Worcestershire sauce,** which the city embraced in the 19th and 20th centuries via European-style restaurants. Ever a place to absorb outside influences, fusion-style dishes, such as this one, sprung up; there was even a popular Shanghai-style borscht. After the 1949 communist revolution, imported Worcestershire sauce became scarce so local brands popped up to fill the gap; some of these are still popular today.

WHERE TO EAT

FENG YU
(上海丰裕生煎(南昌店)
41 Ruijin No 2 Road, Huangpu
黄浦区 瑞金二路41号
6am–8.30pm daily.
A no-frills, no-English eatery that packs with locals on the hunt for their favourite breakfast and lunch snacks (the *shēng jiān bāo* are tops; see page 17). There are over 35 branches around town, all with varying menus but this one (which is state owned) serves a *páigǔ niángāo* that's a satisfying rib-sticker.

XIAN DE LAI
(鲜得来排骨年糕)
36 Yunnan South Road, Huangpu 黄浦区 云南南路 36号 11am–8pm daily.
Order your chop (really more a "steak") with a cleansing bowl of *dan dang* soup (双档或单档) to flush away the grease; this is light and features a pork-stuffed tofu-skin wrap and a fried tofu nub (also filled with minced pork) floating in it.

LAO SHENG XING
(老盛兴汤包馆)
258 Shandong Middle Road, Huangpu
黄浦区 山东中路258号
6am–9pm daily.
Opposite a downtown hospital and always humming, there's a method to the madness here. Line up at the register and order from the illuminated menu above the cashier, pay, then bring your receipt to one of the windows – if you get lost in translation, someone will help. The crispiest, crunchiest pork chop ever is your reward!

FOOD STREETS

In the run up to the 2010 Expo, **Wujiang Road Food Street**
(吴江路小吃街), Shanghai's premier character-filled street food
strip, was shuttered. It's been reborn, in a manner of speaking, but
with plenty of Western and general Asian foods now in the mix. Check
it out by all means; especially the multi-tiered building at No 269,
where you'll find a wide range of snack foods and branches of famous
snack restaurants. Sadly, food streets in-the-raw no longer exist. Yet
there are a few pockets to hit, where snack outlets, humble canteens
and sit-down restaurants are concentrated. Here are some favourites.

BARBECUED SPARROWS
ON STICKS AT
QIBAO OLD STREET

QIBAO OLD STREET 七宝老街

WHERE? In Qibao in the western suburbs of Shanghai, about 18 km from the centre of the city. Access it on Metro Line 9; the train trip takes around 25 minutes.

WHY? It's a suburb of Shanghai now but Qibao, an erstwhile water town, retains a few hints of antique charm in its stone-flagged streets and graceful, arched bridges. Visiting here is a quick way to escape the city, especially on a weekday morning when the streets of Qibao are quiet. Avoid weekends unless you particularly crave the crush of hungry crowds. And we mean crush.

WHAT? Although touristy, Qibao Old Street and the surrounding lanes have some lovely traditional architecture, including temples and teahouses. Food stalls sell a diverse range of treats, from sparrows on sticks (麻雀烧烤), soy-simmered pork knuckles (蹄膀), *tāngyuán* (汤圆), or simmered glutinous rice dumplings, *hǎitáng gāo* (海棠), baked rice cakes with a red bean filling, banana rice in bamboo (泰国香蕉竹), hot pot (火锅), fermented tofu (臭豆腐), beggar's chicken, steamed buns, noodles and more. Arrive feeling adventurous... and hungry. Vendors are packed close together – all you need to do is wander and graze on whatever takes your fancy.

YUNNAN SOUTH ROAD 云南南路

WHERE? Just on the other side of Yan'an Elevated Road (延安高架路), not far from People's Square.

WHY? At any time of the day, there's a meal awaiting. Expect everything from breakfast-hour snacks, such as *shēng jiān bāo* at **Dahuchun** (see page 16), cakes, dumplings and even coffee, through to Peking duck and pork chops with rice cakes (see page 64). In the evening, copper hot pots come out for northern-style coal-fired hot-pot dishes.

WHAT? Aside from the casual, street eats, check out **Deda** (德大西菜社) at No 2, a venerable European-style cafe. The original opened in 1897; it's quaint and frequented by old-timers, who come for the coffee and cakes. **Xiao Shaoxing** (小绍兴) at No 69-75 has been around since 1940. It serves a legendary cold simmered chicken (小绍兴白斩鸡), popular even for breakfast with a side of chicken congee (rice porridge, 鸡粥). **Yan Yun Lou** at No 100 has been serving Shanghailanders its Peking duck (北京烤鸭) since 1921 – and it's very affordable. Staying with the duck theme, **Xiao Jin Ling** (小金陵盐水鸭店) at No 55 is famed for cold Nanjing salted duck (盐水鸭).

Fish balls in hotpot, Qibao

Rice flour cakes

Colourful cakes

Cold simmered chicken

Ducks roasting

Fried fermented tofu

Stuffed lotus roots

Rice and red bean dumplings

Flatbreads, Zhejiang South Road

Snacks, Yunnan Road

Lamb skewers

ZHAPU ROAD 乍浦路

WHERE? In Hongkou District, (虹口区) just over the Suzhou Creek, where few tourists seem to venture.

WHY? It's literally a stroll from Nanjing East Road, but feels like another world entirely. Gritty and uncompromisingly local, here's an adventure you can easily take. Favoured among Chinese as a dining destination, Zhapu Road and the surrounding streets are filled with food and architectural discoveries for the intrepid – there are some wonderful old buildings.

WHAT? It's purely Chinese food on offer, with plenty of sit-down restaurants to choose from. With not much English in evidence, you'll be pointing at your fellow diners' dishes to order – that's half the fun.

Try **Haiwang Restaurant** (海王大酒店) at 130-138 Zhapu Road for a large selection of dishes prepared in traditional Shanghai style, including sweet and sour deep-fried Squirrel Fish (see page 98), salt and pepper beef and roasted turtle. Excellent too is **Xiangmanlou** (香满楼) at No 429, with an equally ripper Shanghainese menu. For a change of food pace, try **Chongqing Chicken Pot** (重庆鸡公煲) at 64 Haining Road (北海宁路64号), just off Zhapu, for spiced-up Sichuan offerings.

ZHEJIANG SOUTH ROAD 浙江南路

WHERE? Parallel to Yunnan South Road, not far from the People's Square end of Nanjing East Road.

WHY? Ramshackle open-air food stalls are becoming a rarity in ever-developing, increasingly-regulated Shanghai. On this small downtown strip, for the time being at least, you can wend your way amid barbecue smoke and watch halal butchers at work. Muslim bakers cook *náng* (馕), large, sesame-encrusted flat breads, in tandoor-like drum ovens. Snack on cumin-encrusted lamb skewers (串儿) and fried beef dumplings (牛肉煎包).

WHAT? Aside from grazing along the street and enjoying the vibe, you can sit in various restaurants by venturing to the middle section of Zhejiang Road. At **Guanguanji Lamian** (贯贯吉拉面), 70 Zhenjiang Middle Road (浙江中路70号), gorge on chewy beef noodles (牛肉拉面) and lamb skewers (烤羊肉串), washed down with red date tea (红枣茶). At Xinjiang **Pamir Restaurant** (帕米尔餐厅), 205 Zhejiang Middle Road (浙江中路205号), you'll get hearty Xinjiang favourites like braised chicken with potatoes and green peppers (大盘鸡) and stewed mutton with *náng* (馕包肉). **Midina** (麦迪娜餐厅) at 205 is well worth a look too; there are even a couple of outside tables and chairs if you fancy braving the downtown air. *

CRAB-BRAISED TOFU AT
DIE YUAN, NEAR XINTIANDI

Let's face it, eating whole crab can be something of a chore. Extricating those sweet nuggets of meat from spindly legs and poking around a carapace, among gills, brain and other sinister bits of crabby offal, is a hassle for the uninitiated. Not to mention a mess-making enterprise.

CRAB-BRAISED TOFU
XIÈFĚN DÒUFU 蟹粉豆腐

Luckily there are plenty of dishes that make a feature of crab flesh, painstakingly picked by nimble-fingered kitchen staff. Asparagus stir-fried with crab meat, crab in egg white omelette, dry noodles with crab meat and mini crab wontons in soup are among the most common.

Then, there's this lush dish, where crab meat and roe are braised gently with pillowy bits of the softest tofu. It's thought to be relatively new to the Chinese culinary repertoire and can also be found beyond Shanghai.

But, as this city is Hairy Crab Central (see page 94), there's no better place to try it. Hairy crabs, with their sensationally rich, yellow roe and sweet, sweet flesh are seasonal *and* highly prized and priced: one hairy crab can cost the minimum daily wage in Shanghai. Some restaurants freight them from Europe during the off-season so they're always on hand for dishes such as this, although other types of crab are also used. ▷

CRAB BRAISED TOFU 蟹粉豆腐

Ingredients are few and simple, so they need to be good. Better places use their own house-made tofu, carefully made stock and a generous quantity of crab. A hint of sautéed onion and ginger and some starch to thicken the stock are among the few other additions.

The texture varies: some versions have a loose, soup-like consistency, while others are gloopier – the result of a heavier hand with thickening agents. The colour varies as well, with brighter yellow-orange examples suggesting an unstinting use of crab roe. ✳

WANG BAO HE
(王宝和大酒店)
603 Fuzhou Road, Huangpu
黄浦区 福州路603号, 近浙江中路
11am – 1.30pm, 5pm – 9pm daily.
This centuries-old institution offers some 80 crab dishes and is also famous for its house brand Shaoxing yellow wine. Wang Bao He pioneered dedicated crab banquet menus in the '80s. Its most expensive crab dish – stir-fried crab flesh packed back into a crab shell – costs 500RMB. For about the same price, try the Crab Feast – a multi-course claw-to-tail extravaganza.

CHOPSTICK ETIQUETTE

Chopsticks are elegant eating implements and their use becomes second nature over time. Here's the rundown on a few dos and don'ts:

✛ Don't shove chopsticks vertically into your food when not using them. This evokes incense sticks in pots of rice on funeral altars. Essentially, it says "death" to Chinese fellow diners.

✛ Don't gesticulate with chopsticks when talking, i.e., resist any temptation to wave them enthusiastically through the air.

✛ Don't skewer your food with chopsticks; don't stab at it with them, either.

✛ It's considered bad form to drop your food when using chopsticks. If the dish is soft, such as crab with tofu, use a spoon to transport it from serving dish to your bowl.

✛ Separating a piece of food into two smaller, mouth-sized pieces using chopsticks involves just one hand to both exert pressure on the chopsticks, while simultaneously moving them apart to break the food. Doing this elegantly is as difficult as it sounds, especially where firm ingredients are involved so... practise.

✛ Double dipping with chopsticks into communal bowls or serving platters of wet dishes is considered unhygienic. Use a serving spoon. Rummaging around a shared dish with your chopsticks, in the hunt for select titbits, is also a no-no.

✛ You can ask for cutlery in a restaurant, although don't expect a knife. They're regarded as instruments of violence in China and generally not used at the table. You'll get a fork and spoon.

WHERE TO EAT

DIE YUAN
(蝶园)
**70 Taicang Road,
near Songshan Road, Huangpu**
黄浦区 太仓路70号
11am–2pm, 6pm–12am daily.
With a menu of local standards, this place fills with Shanghainese diners, not tourists. Which is surprising, given its proximity to flashy Xintiandi. Its crab with tofu is particularly delicious, with the rich colour and flavour that only plenty of roe can bring to the party.

CHENG LONG HANG XIE WANG FU
(成隆行蟹王府)
216 Jiujiang Road, Huangpu
黄浦区 九江路216号
11am–2pm, 5–10pm daily.
Decor is reminiscent of an old Chinese mansion. It has its own crab farm – in season, you can choose your crab live from aquariums out front. Crab with tofu is available in a small portion, allowing room for other crabby treats. At night, live traditional music plays.

LING LONG GE
(凌泷阁)
2F, 951 Hongxu Road, Changning
长宁区 虹许路951号2楼
11am–2pm, 5–10pm daily.
Serving hairy crab year-round from an extensive menu (they import crabs from Holland in the off season), Ling Long Ge has some of Shanghai's most elegant private rooms. As well as a particularly gorgeous crab with tofu, it's famous for its yin yang pastries, made with a half lotus paste, half curried crab filling, and for spicy, roe-spiked *dan dan* noodles.

THE ESSENTIAL HAIRY CRAB

Hairy crabs. Such a fun name, such delectable critters. Don't miss trying these if you're in town in late autumn, when they're at their seasonal peak.

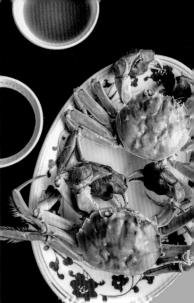

Locals go NUTS for hairy crabs (dàzháxiè 上海大闸蟹). Purists prefer them simply steamed and served whole, crouching on a plate with a mixture of black rice vinegar, sugar and ginger for dipping. Anything else muddies the flavour, they reckon, but that doesn't stop fancy hotel restaurants concocting all manner of haute, hairy-crab-infused menus when these gourmet crustaceans are in season.

The Chinese also reckon female hairy crabs (mǔ máoxiè, 母毛蟹) are at their most delicious point in October, while the males (gon máoxiè, 公毛蟹) hit their peak in November. Males are generally larger, with slightly more meat. Which gender is "best" is the subject of endless gastronomic debate.

The fuss is mostly about the gooey, golden roe of the female crab – ordering one of these babies can stiff you more than a prime steak. Mind you, the milt (aka sperm) of the male is also mighty tasty and prized. ∗

HAIRY CRAB FACTS

✚ The Chinese hairy crab, *Eriocheir sinensis*, is also known as the Chinese mitten crab. In other countries, including parts of Europe, the UK and the USA, it's considered an invasive species. It was introduced to Germany in the 1930s, but the Germans now have a lucrative trade exporting the delicious pests back to China.

✚ Genuine hairy crabs come from Yangcheng Lake, near Suzhou, which has limited production. Most of these go to five-star hotels; crabs from nearby Lake Taihu are cheaper.

✚ The best specimens exhibit a green carapace, a white belly, stout, golden legs and long, gleaming, yellowish leg hair… which almost sounds like something you'd want to date.

✚ The Chinese consider crab meat to have a "cooling" (yin) effect on the body, so it's traditional to serve crab with yellow rice wine, which is "warming" (yang).

✚ It's a mark of great prowess to eat a steamed crab without breaking the exoskeleton, reconstructing it after the meat is extracted. There are no less than eight tools, developed during the Ming dynasty, used to achieve this. First-timers generally end up wearing half their crab's innards, so relax if this happens to you.

✚ Hairy crab taboos include cooking dead crabs, eating raw crabs, eating too much crab at one time (maybe because both the milt and the roe are super-rich in cholesterol) and, curiously, eating crab with persimmons or beer.

✚ Female crabs generally – not just hairy crabs – are said to have sweeter meat than males. You can easily tell the sexes apart: males have a pronounced v-shaped white flap on their underside; the female equivalent is circular.

WHERE TO EAT

LING LONG GE (凌泷阁)
2F 951 Hongxu Road, Changning
长宁区 虹许路951号2楼,
11am–2pm, 5–10pm daily.
Chinese users of Dianping, the online dining guide, flock to this place, dedicated to Yancheng Lake crabs. Try the crab sandwiches.

YI LONG COURT (逸龍閣)
The Peninsula Shanghai
2F, 32 Zhongshan East No 1 Road, Huangpu
黄浦区 中山东一路32号
11.30am–2.30pm,
6–10.30pm daily
One of Shanghai's best restaurants (2 Michelin stars) and certainly the most beautiful. The eight-course crab dinner, for a cool RMB988, is a stunner.

XIN GUANG JIU JIA
(新光酒家)
512 Tianjin Road, Huangpu
黄浦区 天津路512号
11am–2pm, 5–9pm daily.
Specialising in multi-course banquets using pre-picked meat to save you hassle. Popular with locals, there's a 400RMB minimum charge.

CHENG LONG HANG XIE WANG FU
(成隆行蟹王府)
216 Jiujiang Road, Huangpu
黄浦区 九江路216号
11am–2pm, 5–10pm daily.
Apart from the steamed, pre-shelled crabs, stupendous crab roe soup dumplings (蟹粉小笼包) are the go here – the broth is deliciously rich with roe.

SHANGHAI'S LARGEST
LION'S HEAD MEATBALL,
AT HONG QI LIN

Poetically named lion's head meatballs come in two distinct varieties: the Yangzhou sort, and the "red-cooked" type. Both versions are cooked with Chinese cabbage leaves or another leafy green – these are what give lion's heads their "mane."

LION'S HEAD MEATBALLS
SHĪZI TÓU 狮子头

Good lion's head meatballs are made using fatty pork that's hand-chopped until very fine, almost like mince. Sometimes water chestnuts or shiitake mushrooms are added for textural interest. But it's the laborious hand-cutting of the meat that makes them so impossibly light – they literally fall apart at the mere suspicion of a chopstick. Good ones should be soft, melting and unctuous, and have a slightly rough surface. This signifies they've been made by hand, not machine.

Red-cooked (*hóngshāo*, 红烧) meatballs are simmered in soy sauce, Shaoxing wine and sugar. The result is dark, glossy and lip-smackingly delicious, demonstrating the local predilection for sweet stickiness. The plainer Yangzhou lion's heads are cooked and served in a stock of incredibly deep, rich flavour and clarity, which as much a delicious treat in its own right as is the meatball itself. ▷

LION'S HEAD MEATBALLS 狮子头

Lion's heads appear on menus throughout the city in humble canteens, and at more polished establishments, too. Their size varies dramatically, from fist-large to that of an oversized golf ball. Generally, a serve is one per person, so stipulate how many you want when ordering.

FYI, lion's heads are said to have been created during the Sui dynasty (589-618). Back then, cooking large pieces of meat was de rigueur, so the concept of meatballs made from tiny bits of chopped meat was considered somewhat revolutionary. ✳

Tai Sheng Yuan, on a busy corner of Huanghe Road

Yangzhou Fandian

WHERE TO EAT

HONG QI LIN (洪齐林老镇)
727 Anyuan Road, Jing'an
静安区 安远路727-2号
11am–2pm, 5–10pm daily.
Reputed to serve the city's largest lion's head meatballs, they arrive on the table glossed in plenty of burnished, starch-thickened red sauce. Hong Qi Lin is a simple place with no English and rudimentary decor, but the staff is mighty friendly. It also does a mean red cooked pork, yellow croaker fish cooked with scrambled eggs (赛螃蟹), and fried rice with preserved pork and seasonal greens (上海菜饭) too.

YANGZHOU FANDIAN (扬州饭店)
345 Fujian Middle Road, Huangpu
黄浦区 福建中路345号
11am–9pm daily
An old-school establishment handy to Nanjing East Road, serving classic Huaiyang Cuisine (淮阳菜). As well as meatballs, try eight treasures in spicy sauce (bā bǎo làjiàng, 宝辣酱), a Yangzte River dish featuring peanuts, peas, bamboo and prawns in a hot sauce that's a home-style classic.

MEILONGZHEN (梅龙镇酒家)
No. 22, Lane 1081, Nanjing West Road, Jing'an
静安区 南京西路1081弄22号
11am–1.30pm, 5–9pm daily.
Around since the 1930s, the grand, traditionally decked-out interiors are glitzy, with seven dining halls and room for 600 diners. The menu embraces Sichuan as well as Yangzhou and Shanghai fare. Check out other local specialities, such as fried eel (响油鳝丝) and crystal prawns (水晶虾仁).

LU BO LANG (上海绿波廊, 豫园路店)
115 Yuyuan Road, Huangpu
黄浦区 豫园路115号
11am–2pm, 5–11pm daily.
There's arguably better food in town, but the convenience of the location, the bright friendliness of the staff and the easily navigated menu make it an excellent pit-stop. The Yangzhou-style lion's heads are especially delicious, with their tasty, meaty stock.

TAI SHENG YUAN (苔圣园, 黄浦店)
50 Huanghe Road, Huangpu
黄浦区 黄河路50号
10.30am–4am daily.
Another large, easy-to-take restaurant, this one's on a prominent corner on Huanghe Road, a famous food street. The historic building is gorgeous, as is the mesmerising goldfish tank in the reception area. Expect the usual array of Shanghainese favourites, with a more petite lion's head on offer, cooked in the Yangzhou fashion.

DIAN SHI ZHAI (点石斋小宴)
320 Yongjia Road, Xuhui
徐汇区 永嘉路320号(近襄阳南路)
11am–2pm, 5.30–9.30pm daily.
Charmingly homey, this mid-range eatery in a 1930s mansion delivers a menu of by-the-book standards. In season, their take on the lion's head comes in a hairy-crab-spiked sauce.

‘ A good lion's head should be "肥而不腻", or rich in fat without being greasy. ’

A leading restaurateur, consultant, author, online food retailer and general mover-and-shaker, JEREME LEUNG is watched by an audience of more than 100 million as a judge on *Masterchef China*. Native to Hong Kong, he's made Shanghai his home and what he doesn't know about the city's food scene isn't worth knowing. One of the most famous food guys in the country, here he shares some of his dining-out faves.

JEREME LEUNG
IS A MASTERCHEF CHINA
JUDGE AND GO-TO GUY ON
DINING IN SHANGHAI

NANLU ZHELI
(南麓.浙里)
216 Sichuan Middle Road, Huangpu
黄浦区 四川中路216号
"Located near the Bund in a heritage building, the lovely interior still has elements of old Shanghai. The beautiful coloured glass and old furniture are like stepping into the art deco era. The cuisine is primarily classic Shanghainese – I'd recommend their red-braised pork (金牌扣肉), carp in golden broth (金汤鲫鱼), and eight treasure rice (八宝辣酱年糕)."

XIN RONG JI
(新荣记)
5F Shanghai Plaza, 138 Huaihai Road, Huangpu
黄浦区 淮海中路138号
无限度广5楼
"This Michelin-starred restaurant serves classic Taizhou [a city 300km south of Shanghai] cuisine. Their must-order dishes include sea worm with green pea-starch noodles (沙蒜烧豆面), pan-fried hairtail fish (干煎带鱼) and braised tofu casserole (家乡手撕豆腐)."

DONG TIAN SHI FU
(洞天食府)
240 Beida Street, Zhujiajiao
朱家角 北大街240号
"Located in Zhujiajiao, about an hour away from Shanghai, and one of the historic old water villages in the area. I recommend their free-range chicken soup (草鸡), water caltrop with hairy bean (菱角毛豆), best in autumn, and river snails stuffed with pork (田螺塞肉)."

OLD JESSE
(老吉士)
41 Tian Ping Road, Xuhui
徐汇区 天平路41号
"An iconic Shanghai restaurant that's been around a long time. Giant halibut fish head cooked in onions (鸦片鱼头), glutinous rice-stuffed red dates (心太软) and red braised pork (红烧肉) are among the must-order dishes." (Also see pages 61, 111)

NANJING DA PAI DANG
(南京大牌档)
3F Shimao Shangdu, No.258 Nanjing West Road, Huangpu
黄浦区 南京西路258号
世茂商都3楼
"A popular Nanjing restaurant chain. The ambience is great – the interior is decorated like a food market and they serve from various open kitchens. Performers sing Suzhou opera every evening. Try their Nanjing-style salted duck (招牌盐水鸭), spicy duck's blood pudding (麻辣鸭血) and lion's head meatballs (清炖狮子头)."

ANTHOLOGIA
(地球美食剧场)
Room 105-107, Building 6, 381 Fanyu Road, Changning
长宁区 番禺路381号6号
楼105-107室
"A modern Japanese restaurant that cooks a strictly set menu of eight courses. The presentation has a strong visual element and the entire restaurant is set up like a theatre. It's a unique dining experience, but you'll need to get your hotel to make a booking for you – there are only 46 seats."

> ' I think one of the most unique aspects of Shanghai is its readiness to embrace new things from every part of China and the globe. In this city, you can find almost anything when it comes to food. There are different styles of Chinese cuisine... then there's Icelandic, Russian, avant-garde fine dining, tapas... We have the best high-end Western cuisines of anywhere in Asia. But tourists should really dine on unique 'Shanghai classics,' dishes like *xiǎo lóng bāo* red braised pork, lion's head dumplings, hairy crabs in autumn etc. Hairy crab is one thing I make a point to eat when they're in season.

A unique masterpiece of Chinese haute cuisine that you mustn't miss, beggar's chicken can be hard to find as not everyone makes it. When you see what goes into its preparation, you'll grasp why and trust us – an appreciation of the assembly is as much to do with enjoying beggar's chicken as is eating the delicious end product. Read on.

BEGGAR'S CHICKEN
JIÀO HUĀ JĪ 叫花鸡

Beggar's chicken originated, legend has it, in Hangzhou. This blissful city near Shanghai is celebrated for its bucolic, lakeside scenery and misty rolling hills, verdant with plantations of the vaunted dragon well (*lóngjǐng*) tea. Achingly beautiful, Hangzhou has a memorable cuisine of its own and you might see some of these dishes on menus around Shanghai: West Lake vinegar fish, Dongpo pork and *lóngjǐng* tea prawns, for example.

Beggar's chicken dates from the Qing dynasty when, the story goes, a famished beggar stole a chicken from a farm. The incensed farmer caught wind of the dastardly deed and chased the robber along a river bank where the enterprising crook hid the bird in mud. Later, he retrieved the bird and cooked it over a wood-fuelled fire, still encased in mud, which formed a hard crust around the chicken. When cracked open, the feathers and skin came away with the clay and the flesh was juicy and ▷

BEGGAR'S CHICKEN 叫花鸡

flavoursome, literally falling off the bones. Coincidentally, the Chinese emperor just happened to saunter by at the precise moment the beggar sat to eat. He tried the chicken, pronounced it fit for the Imperial Court menu and the rest, as they say, is culinary history.

These days the dish isn't very beggar-y, having taken on a number of refinements. It's also not cheap to order, with a good B.C., serving two, setting you back around 300 RMB.

Preparing the bird involves marinating in soy, Shaoxing wine and spices, then stuffing with a savoury mixture, the composition of which varies. Chopped pork, raw-cured Jinhua ham, preserved vegetables, gingko nuts, fresh chestnuts and varieties of mushrooms are typical. Unsurprisingly, the better the restaurant, the higher the quality of ingredients used and the more complex the flavour. Before enclosing it in a thin layer of clay, (which is non-toxic and, for complete authenticity, should be sourced from Hangzhou), the whole stuffed bird is wrapped first in lotus leaves and then in baking parchment or cellophane. Looking for all the world like a large rock, the parcelled up, clay-covered bird is baked at a high temperature in a wood-fired oven. To serve, the clay crust is cracked open at the table (sometimes the exterior is flamed

Wrapping the bird, Xindalu

Cooked stuffing

Flaming at table

first in alcohol) using a wooden mallet. Inside, the chicken has cooked to succulent perfection, with flavours, juices and aromas trapped inside its clay sarcophagus, which acts like a mini-oven. Labour-intensive beggar's chicken generally requires advance ordering, as it takes some six hours to prepare. *

Stuffing ingredients: Xindalu

" Beggar's chicken dates from the Qing dynasty when, the story goes, a famished beggar stole a chicken from a farm. "

WHERE TO EAT

XINDALU
(新大陆中国厨房)
Hyatt On The Bund, 199 Huangpu Road, Hongkou
黄浦路199号上海外滩茂悦大酒店东楼大堂
11.30am–2.30pm, 5.30–10.30pm daily.
Order ahead to secure a bird. It will be stuffed with, among other things, a selection of exotic fresh mushrooms, many flown in from Yunnan province in China's extreme south west. This is one of Shanghai's best restaurants; the food is exceptional, with a menu showcasing the cuisine of the lower Yangtze region.

HAI PAI
(海派)
Andaz Hotel, 88 Songshan Road, Xintiandi
黄浦区 嵩山路88号新天地安达仕酒店
11.30am–2.30pm, 5.30–10.30pm daily.
At this seasonally driven restaurant, cross fingers chef Qiu has her osmanthus-scented, abalone-stuffed beggar's chicken on the menu when you visit. It is sealed with egg white and broken open at the table. The remaining fare is home-style Chinese but served with elegant, modern twists. In keeping with this, the interior is bright, breezy and markedly contemporary.

WANGSI
(王四酒家)
2F, 18 Xizang Middle Road, Huangpu
黄浦区 西藏中路18号 2楼
11.30am–2.30pm, 5.30–10pm daily.
A more affordable beggar's chook, and excellent it is too. Wangsi has been a part of the Shanghai dining scene since the Qing dynasty. It's a chain now, but still family owned and popular with local diners. It serves its B.C. with a generous side of pork and the whole thing could easily fill three diners.

AI MEI
(艾美轩中餐厅)
8F, Le Royal Meridien Shanghai,
789 East Nanjing Road, Huangpu
黄浦区 南京东路789号世茂皇家艾美酒店.
11.30am–2.30pm, 5.30–10pm daily.
The bird used here is the famous Wenchang chicken from Hainan Island. Marinated in warm, aromatic spices, the pastry crust is a departure from the traditional clay but the results are deliciously memorable. The room, complete with an immense arch-shaped aquarium and views over People's Park, is impressive.

A day trip to Suzhou

Suzhou is connected to Shanghai by a 200km-an-hour-plus fast-train ride that takes around 25 minutes. Yes, that's right – the city that's famed worldwide for classical Chinese gardens is now practically a suburb of Shanghai. As such, it makes for a perfect day trip from the Big Smoke, although frankly you could easily fill three or four days here.

THE HUMBLE ADMINISTRATOR'S GARDEN A CLASSICAL CHINESE GARDEN

PRAWNS COOKED
WITH *BÌLUÓCHŪN* TEA
AT WUMEN RENJIA

A DAY TRIP TO SUZHOU

The Lingering Garden

Green tea cakes

Shantang Street

With a population of around 4 million, **Suzhou** (苏州) is hardly a small place. But if a day is all you've got, no worries; **here are some ideas for a busy eight-hour itinerary** that will give a taste of the place. Taxis are the best way to get around, although they can be scarce at peak times. Pedicabs ply main tourist areas and although slower and more exxie, they're a handy option. Arrive hungry; this town has some famous eats.

7.30am

Head to **Zhu Hong Xing** for breakfast and order their fine "dragon-beard" (龙须面) noodles. Suzhou cuisine makes an art of stewing and simmering and any dishes involving stock, such as soup noodles (汤面), are knock-out. If dumplings are more your speed, try **Yangyang Dumplings** for the legendary porky bites the locals clamour for. Their fried pork and coriander dumplings are a favourite, but chive-egg and crabmeat-green vegetable ones are also excellent. The huge menu offers much more besides dumplings.

Suzhou's elegant gardens draw visitors from over the globe, with eight on UNESCO's cultural heritage list. Arrive early as they become exceptionally crowded. **The Humble Administrator's Garden** is over 500 years old and by far the largest. It, **The Lingering Garden** and **Master Of Nets Garden** are all breathtaking show-stoppers, with pavilions, pools, bridges, rockeries and waterfalls-aplenty.

10.30am

Clinging to the side of the canal on picturesque, pedestrianised **Pinjiang Road** ((平江路), **Pin Von Teahouse** is a popular venue. Order local snacks from the illustrated menu; the divine "sugar" porridge (糖粥), made from glutinous rice and red bean paste, or crisp green tea cakes (西山碧螺茶饼), for example. The tea cakes are squished together with sweetened taro puree, studded with sesame seeds and are extremely moreish. Wash them down with the local brew of choice, green *biluóchūn* tea (碧螺春), grown in the region.

The 1km-long Pinjiang Road is quaint and it's the launch-pad for 45-minute man-powered boat rides around Suzhou's canals. The songs of the boatmen, an emblematic sound of Suzhou, fill the air. Walkable from Pinjiang Road is the small, beautifully proportioned **Couples Retreat Garden,** a low-key option to some of the more heavily subscribed gardens in town. ▷

12.00pm

Grab a cab to **Xiyuan temple,** celebrated for its collection of more than 800 Buddhist sculptures, stands of ancient trees, gardens, pavilions, arhat halls and long corridors. The presence of turtles in the beautiful, fish-filled Fangsheng Pond is said to date from the Ming Dynasty.

Wumen Renjia, near the Lion Grove Garden and right next to the delightful **Suzhou Folk Custom Museum,** is a stalwart of local cuisine. The interior is dreamy and the cooks are scrupulous with their ingredients, choosing only the seasonal best. It's hard to find pure, Suzhou cooking like this these days. Prawns cooked with *biluóchūn* tea (碧螺春虾仁) is a speciality and, in season (around October), they feature water vegetables (lotus root, water caltrop and water chestnuts) harvested from nearby Taihu Lake, in dishes.

Suzhou is known for silk production and the **Suzhou No 1 Silk Factory** is fascinating. You will probably want to purchase an affordable silk-filled duvet or two, designed to cope with both sticky summer heat and the bone-chill of a Suzhou winter. The tranquil **I.M.Pei designed Suzhou Museum** is crammed with ceramics, calligraphy, crafts, paintings and other treasures from the Wu Kingdom, of which Suzhou was the major hub. The sublime building is drenched in natural light and features a garden and pool out the back.

2.30pm

Walking up **Guanqian Road,** (观前街), the main retail hub of Suzhou, is mandatory. It's a great place to pick up mementos, such as celebrated Suzhou silk embroideries, fans, jade pieces and tea. **Ye Shou He** dates from 1870 and specializes in Suzhou candies. The local sweet tooth is legendary and can best be seen in action at **Huang Tian Yuan** where fresh rice cakes and pastries come in over 320 mind-boggling varieties. Snack along **Taijian Lane,** (太监弄) where dozens of stalls proffer everything from fried fermented (or "stinky") tofu (臭豆腐), steamed dim sum, freshwater crayfish (小龙虾) and rice-stuffed lotus root (糯米藕) cooked in sweet syrup and scented with osmanthus flowers.

4.00pm

The 1,100 year old **Shantang Street,** (金阊区山塘街), in Gusu District, is another historic precinct punctuated by quaint arched bridges, meandering canal ways and pretty cobbled streets. Shops are a tad main-stream but, with plenty of lantern-festooned facades, the place maintains a party atmosphere. There are some terrific eateries; try the branch of famous restaurant **Song He Lou**. The bean curd with crab roe and Suzhou whitebait soup are killer. Adjoining streets make for a pleasant stroll, when the lanterns come on and crowds thin. ✳

STUFFED LOTUS ROOT,
SNACKS AND TEA
AT PIN VON TEAHOUSE

A DAY TRIP TO SUZHOU

The Humble Administrator's Garden

Temple, Guanxian Street

Wumen Renjia

Dim sum, Taijian Lane

Master of The Nets Garden

Dragon beard noodles

DAY TRIP DIRECTORY

THE HUMBLE ADMINISTRATOR'S GARDEN (拙政园)
178 Dongbei Road
东北街178号
7.30am–5.30pm daily

THE LINGERING GARDEN (留园)
338 Liyuan Road
留园路338号
7.30am–5pm daily

MASTER OF THE NETS GARDEN (网师园)
11 Kuojiatou Road
沧浪区带城桥路北阔家头巷11号
7.30am–5.30pm daily

SUZHOU FOLK MUSEUM
(苏州民俗博物馆)
32 Panru Alley
平江区潘儒巷32号
8am–4.30pm daily

ZHU HONG XING NOODLE SHOP
(朱鸿兴面馆 观前店)
108 Gong Xiang
苏州市平江区宫巷108号(碧凤坊口)
6am–10pm daily

YANGYANG DUMPLINGS
(洋洋饺子馆)
420 Shiquan Street
沧浪区十全街420号
9am–1am daily

WUMEN RENJIA
(吴门人家, 潘儒巷店)
31 Panruxian Road
平江区潘儒巷31号
拙政园附近
11am–2.30pm,
5pm–8.30pm daily

PIN VON TEAHOUSE
(品芳斋)
94 Pingjian Road
平江号94号
10am–9pm daily

COUPLES RETREAT GARDEN (耦园)
6 Xiaoxing Alley
小新桥巷6号
7.15am–5pm daily

XIYUAN TEMPLE
(苏州西园寺)
18 Xiyuan Lane
金阊区留园路西园弄18号
7.30am–5.30pm

SUZHOU NO 1 SILK FACTORY
(苏州第一丝厂)
94 Nanmen Road
沧浪区南门路94号
9am–6pm daily

SUZHOU MUSEUM
(蘇州博物館)
204 Dongbei Street
平江区东北街204号
9am–5pm (closed Mon)

YE SHOU HE
(叶受和)
69 Guanqian Street
观前街69号
8.30am–9pm daily

HUANG TIAN YUAN
(黄天源)
86 Guanqian Street
观前街86号东脚门
8.30am–9.30pm daily

SONG HE LOU
(松鹤楼)
198 Shantang Street
山塘街198号
11am–1.30pm,
5–8:30pm daily

AT NANLING
RESTAURANT, UPSTAIRS
IN THE VAST JING'AN
JIALI CENTER

Piscine critters are an important part of Shanghai cuisine and come from all watery environs — sea, lakes and rivers. Freshness and flavour are highly prized so fish tend to be cooked and served whole. So steel yourself for shells, heads, eyes, bones and tails at the table. The full catastrophe.

SQUIRREL-SHAPED MANDARIN FISH

SŌNGSHŬ YÚ 松鼠鱼

Many of Shanghai's famous fishy dishes are from nearby cities. Steamed custard with cockles (蛤蜊蒸蛋) for example, is from Ningbo, a coastal city near the Zhoushan Archipelago, one of Chinas largest fisheries. Then there's fried yellow croaker fish with green onions (竹网葱香小鱼), also from Ningbo. The version at **Jian Guo 328** (see page 63) is sensational. **Old Jesse** (see pages 61, 85, 111) is famous for *cōng shāo yú tóu* (鸦片鱼头) which is similar, but made using a whole fish head roasted in the onions. It needs to be pre-ordered and is one of town's most cult-followed fish dishes.

Perhaps the most famous imported fish dish is squirrel-shaped mandarin fish, from Suzhou. Its origins are traced to the times of Emperor Qianlong, who purportedly tasted the dish while dining at **Song He Lou** restaurant in Suzhou in the 1700s. (The restaurant still exists though not in original form; see page 97). Everyone loves the crunchy fried exterior, the juicy nublets ▷

SQUIRREL-SHAPED MANDARIN FISH 松鼠鱼

of flesh and the moreish sweet-and-sour coating sauce. Served whole, the spine and most of the bones are removed before cooking, making the flesh easy to eat. It's scored through the skin in a fine network of cuts that open out spectacularly as the fish fries; considerable skill is required for this knife work. The sauce is made from sugar, red vinegar, stock and tomato ketchup, and thickened with starch. Peas, pine nuts and small prawns form a common, but by no means standard, garnish. With its gaping mouth and curled tail, it's always a dramatic dish.

Mandarin fish at Shanghai Ren Jia

The name comes from the shape of the finished dish, which is said to resemble a furry animal on the plate, with its tail bent upward and the fine spikes of flesh representing the coat (some imagination is required). Other explanations claim that the fish makes a squirrel-like squeaking sound when the hot sauce is poured over the fresh-from-the-fryer flesh.

The fish most commonly used for this dish is guì yú (桂鱼), a species of freshwater perch that can grow up to 70cm long and is revered for its fine flavour and texture. Experts claim freshwater fish are in their prime during April and May when they're getting more active after winter, building muscle and flavour. ∗

Dining room at Nanling

POPULAR FISH VARIETIES

+ **PERCH** (*lú yú*, 鲈鱼)
A good option for bone haters with its excellent, mild flavour, medium-firm texture and easily navigable bone structure.

+ **YELLOW CROAKER** (*huánghuā yú*, 黄花鱼)
A versatile, but bony, salt-water fish with sweet, flaky white meat. You'll encounter it a lot on menus.

+ **HAIRTAIL FISH** (*píng yú*, 平鱼)
A great option for the cost-conscious. It's on many restaurant menus but its boniness can be a drawback.

+ **POMFRET** (*chāng yú*, 平鱼) A good-eating flat fish with lovely, firm flesh and easily removed bones.

+ **CARP** (*lǐyú*, 鲤鱼)
Farmed in China for thousands of years. Well-raised, it has a delicate flavour; if it tastes muddy it has not been kept in fresh water. Some types of carp are red cooked; look for *hóngshāo huá shu* (红烧划水) on menus.

+ **RIVER EEL** (*hé mán*, 河鳗) Synonymous with Shanghai. As well as eel noodles (see page 44), *xiǎng yóu shàn hu* (响油鳝糊), it's the most famed Shanghai eel dish. It's stir-fried with ginger, sugar, bamboo, soybean sauce and yellow wine. At the table, boiling oil is poured over and the whole thing sizzles.

SQUIRREL-SHAPED MANDARIN FISH 松鼠鱼

WHERE TO EAT

SHANGHAI CHIC (上海会馆)
5F, 489 Henan Road, Huangpu
黄浦区 河南南路489号5楼
11am–9.30pm daily.
Handily located near Nanjing East Road and People's Square in an upmarket mall. As well as featuring mandarin fish, the menu is a roll-call of all the sweet, hearty, delicious dishes Shanghai is so famous for.

LYNN MODERN (琳怡)
99 Xikang Road, Jing'an
静安区 西康路99号
11.30am–2.30pm, 6–10.30pm daily.
A long-time stalwart, Lynn serves stellar Shanghainese faves with a slight Cantonese lean and in a smart setting. Its fantastic mandarin fish is just part of the story – dim sum lovers should take note of the weekend all-you-can-eat dim sum deal.

SHANGHAI REN JIA (上海人家)
41 Yunnan Middle Road, Huangpu
黄浦区 云南中路 41号
11am–9pm daily.
Good-value Shanghai food in a restaurant with an authentic vibe – staff are a little bemused by tourist clientele. The fresh seafood cooking station is a winner, as are the hairy crabs in wine, in season. Oh and the mandarin fish too, natch.

SHUN FENG (顺风大酒店)
3F Central Plaza, 227 Huangpi North Road, Huangpu
陂北路227号中区广场3楼
11am–2pm, 5–10pm daily.
Chattery crowds, some Hangzhou specialities, plenty of dim sum, good fish-cooking and a spacious dining room (with some natural light) make this place, near People's Park, a sure-fire choice. Order the rice dessert (see page 121).

NANLING (南伶酒家)
S3-01 Jing'an Jiali Center, 1238 Yan'an Middle Road, Jing'an
静安区 延安中路1238号静安嘉里中心南区商场S3-01
11am–2pm, 5.30–10pm daily.
Set in a swish shopping centre, this stylish, contemporary restaurant hums at peak times. It can get noisy! The squirrel-shaped mandarin fish here is a few cuts above, with nifty knife work and a not-so-cloying sauce. The cold appetisers here are particularly elegant.

Bars with KILLER views

With one of the world's most distinctive metropolitan skylines, plus a nightly light show sparking up Pudong with raucous, flashing colours, you'll want to soak up all of Shanghai's sparkle. Having a drink at hand makes the spectacle extra compelling — not to mention more chillaxing, particularly after a day spent pounding the throbbing streets. Here's where to head for a bar-side seat.

FRONT-ROW SEATS TO
THE BEST VIEWS IN TOWN
AT THE FELLAS

BARS WITH KILLER VIEWS

VUE BAR Hyatt on the Bund
32-33F, 199 Huangpu Road, Hongkou
黄浦路199号, 外滩茂悦大酒32-33楼 近武昌路 5.30pm–1am daily.

Take in views from a loungy day bed, or even the jacuzzi, which the rich-kid clientele love cavorting in during summer. A circular cocktail bar is the focus of the 32nd floor; brilliant interiors are the work of legendary Tokyo firm Super Potato. Sitting above a strategic bend in the Huangpu, the unimpeded vistas over the eccentric Pudong skyline and the full sweep of the Bund are fabulous.

MANGO AND BERRY
COCKTAILS AT VUE BAR

THE FELLAS ▶

7F, 7 Yanan East Road, Huangpu
黄浦区 延安东路7号7楼 近中山东一路
5pm–2am daily.

The Fellas mixes some of town's best drinks, some using local spirits. The Ancient Smoky Secret (right) arrives with full drama under a glass cloche and features Chinese bitters, Campari and vermouth. The Chinglish, a fusion of rum, melon liqueur, lychee, lemon and baiju, is similarly stunning. Score a seat on the L-shaped terrace, but be prepared to move if you haven't reserved, as it's a wildly popular perch for the well-heeled regulars.

EPICURE on 45

Radisson Blu Hotel
88 Nanjing West Road, Huangpu
黄浦区 南京西路88号 **11.30am–2.30pm, 6–10.30pm daily.**

A brilliant place to watch Shanghai spin by, way, way below. The restaurant completes a full revolution every 90 minutes and the quirky Radisson building, which dominates the area, has good proximity to People's Square.

◀ SIR ELLY'S TERRACE

The Peninsula Shanghai
14F, 32 Zhongshan East No 1 Road, Huangpu
黄浦区 中山东一路32号13楼
5pm–12am Sun–Thurs,
5pm–1am Fri–Sat.

This open-air bar is one for the movers and shakers, with its dress-circle location, amazing 14th-floor vistas of the Bund and impeccable service. The champagne cocktails are signature drinks.

BARS WITH KILLER VIEWS

TOPS BAR ▶
Banyan Tree Shanghai on The Bund, 13F, 19 Gongping Road, Hongkou 虹口区 公平路19号13楼 2.30pm–1am Mon–Thurs, 11am–2.00am Fri–Sat, 11am–1.00am Sun.

Shanghai's celebs and groovy set decamp here of an afternoon, chowing down on high tea and taking selfies in front of the breathtaking view. The panoramic sweep of the Bund is spectacular from here.

SWATCH ART PEACE HOTEL
6F, 23 Nanjing East Road, Huangpu 黄浦区 南京东路23号-6楼 5.30pm–12am daily.

The uninterrupted views over to the Pearl Tower and Pudong are stunning, as are the signature martinis. Some trivia for Chinese history buffs: Chiang Kai-shek and Soong Mei-ling celebrated their engagement here in 1927.

M ON THE BUND
7F, 20 Guangdong Road (cnr 5 Zhongshan East 1st Road), Huangpu 黄浦区 广东路20号 (外滩5号)7楼 6.15pm–10.30pm Mon–Fri, 11.30am–5pm and 6.15–10:30pm Sat–Sun.

A cheat entry, as M's terrace is part of their restaurant, not a dedicated bar, per se. Set at the southern end of the Bund, the views that trail up the Bund's majestic curve are compelling, as is the feeling the you're right amongst the impressive, landmark buildings. Come on a sunny weekend when they serve casual brunch, with a cocktail included in the cover price.

DINING ROOM
Park Hyatt, 91F, 100 Century Avenue, Pudong
浦东新区 世纪大道100号环球金融中心内91楼 6am–12am daily

Views skim over the 88-storey Jin Mao tower, one of Shanghai's most emblematic buildings. They extend all the way to the far reaches of Puxi, as far as the eye can see – or the air quality will allow. The vibe is chilled and unpretentious; during the day there are people reading books, families dining and groups sipping tea. For more glamour, whiz up to the Shanghai Lounge, a cozy 60-seater on the floor above. ✳

AT SHANGHAI
GRANDMOTHER, A DINING
SCENE STALWART

The swine looms large on the Shanghai table. If there's one dish that best illustrates the local devotion to all things porcine (meat, fat, skin and all), it's *hóngshāo ròu*. Lip-smacking and lustrous, with deep flavours and the melting-est of textures, you'll dream of it long after you fly home.

RED-COOKED PORK
HÓNGSHĀO RÒU 红烧肉

"Red cooking" is a signature technique of Shanghai cuisine, where ingredients are braised in a mixture of Shaoxing wine, soy sauce, sugar, ginger and aromatics (star anise, fennel seeds and cassia bark, for example). The name is for the colour of the finished dish, which is sometimes boosted by powdered red yeast rice, a natural colourant also used to give lustre to Chinese barbecue meats. Fish, chicken, eel, duck and even eggplant can be red-cooked, but it's in pork that it arguably finds its apogee.

Some restaurants cook pork shoulder, others the trotters, others the knuckle. But belly, called "five flower meat" (五花肉) after the alternating layers of lean and fat, is always the stand-out. Boiled eggs, knots of hard tofu, salted fish, green peppers, cuttlefish or bamboo shoots are often added. The braising liquid reduces to a ▷

> **'Don't even think of prising off the wobbly, lip-smacking layers of skin and fat. That's just plain wrong.'**

Pork being served Ye Shanghai

thick, glistening puddle that cloaks the meat and gives every mouthful an unctuous, sweet and savoury tang. You need steamed rice, a simple veg dish and a stiff walk afterwards to counteract the decadent richness.

Not wholly unique to Shanghai, versions of red-cooked pork are found country-wide. The dish was a favourite of Chairman Mao, who hailed from Hunan Province. ✱

PORCINE TRIVIA

✚ The pig was first domesticated in China, around 4900 BC.

✚ It's thought that the character for "home" (家) developed as a pictograph of a roof over a pig.

✚ Each Chinese person eats around 40kg of pork per year, based on 2014 studies – five times more than they ate in 1979.

✚ The Chinese government keeps a Pork Reserve to ensure the meat remains available and affordable at all times.

✚ The pig is one of the animals in the Chinese zodiac and represents tolerance and optimism.

✚ Half of the world's pigs, about 476 million, are said to reside in China, according to the Earth Policy Institute (2012).

WHERE TO EAT

SHANGHAI GRANDMOTHER
(上海姥姥)
70 Fuzhou Road, Huangpu
黄浦区 福州路70号
11am–2.30pm, 4.30–10pm daily.
A solid option near Nanjing East Road, with an English menu and well priced, authentic meals across the gamut. The red-cooked pork with hard-boiled eggs is brilliant.

OLD JESSE
(吉士酒家)
41 Tian Ping Road, Xuhui
徐汇区 天平路41号
10am–4pm, 5.30pm–12.00am daily.
One of the most famed restaurants in town, it's even listed in the Michelin guide. It's shabby but clean with tables that are hard to score (booking ahead is a must) and not much English spoken. Worth any and every inconvenience.

1221
1221 Yan'an West Road, Jing'an
静安区 延安西路122号,
11.30am–2pm, 5.30–11pm daily.
A long-standing favourite with ex-pats, with its tucked-away location, chic decor, English-speaking staff and refined renditions of all the Shanghai standards which include red-cooked pork.

YE SHANGHAI
(夜上海)
338 Huangpu South Road, Xintiandi
黄浦区 黄陂南路338号
11.30am–2.30pm, 5.30–10.30pm daily.
An upmarket restaurant in Xintiandi with serene interiors and cracking service. The braised pork knuckle in soy veers a little off the usual red-cooked path, but is freaking delish.

LAN XIN
(兰心餐厅)
130 Jinxing Road, Huangpu
黄浦区 进贤路130号
10am–9.00pm daily.
The street's getting trendier by the moment, but this weeny family-run joint is resisting modernisation. Its red-cooked pork is legendary. Don't be put off by the unremarkable appearance – it's a favourite of songstress Faye Wong, no less.

HAI JIN ZI
(海金滋)
240 Jinxing Road, Xuhui
徐汇区 进贤路240号
11am–1.45pm, 5–9.30pm daily.
Another buzzy, old-style canteen on Jinxing Road. Food is particularly cheap and authentic, but staff can be a touch blustery. As well as the pork, the crab roe scrambled eggs (蟹粉蛋) is sublime.

WHERE TO WALK THE PORK OFF

When you've had one dumpling too many (and who hasn't?) it's time for an invigorating stroll. Ranking fourth among cities world-wide with the highest number of skyscrapers, Shanghai is dense with glass, steel, asphalt and crowded pavements. Yet despite that, it's possible to find lovely spots to walk. From tranquil parks to walkways that wind through dense, *Blade Runner*-esque cityscapes, hunt out these options.

JING'AN SCULPTURE PARK
Urban Fox by Alex Rinsler

JING'AN SCULPTURE PARK 静安雕塑公园

Breathe the air, revel in the green, green grass (up to a point – you can't walk on it) and marvel at the sculptural masterpieces in this 45 hectare haven just off Beijing West Road. The sculptural exhibits, which come from 61 world cities, were unveiled in 2010 for the Shanghai World Expo. You won't miss *Red Beacon*, an imposing architectural piece by Belgian Arne Quinze comprising 55 tonnes of wood that form a wondrous canopy-like structure. Alex Rinsler's seven-metre-high *Urban Fox*, sitting on a red shipping container, is striking. There are over 300 large trees in the park, including cherry, camphor, gingko and beech. Access the park from the Nanjing Road West Station on Line 1 – it's about a 10-minute walk away.

JING'AN SCULPTURE PARK

Shattered Spheres by Brent Comber

WALK THE PORK OFF
PEOPLE'S PARK 人民公园

People's Park provides respite from the relentless argy-bargy of nearby Nanjing East Road and the adjacent People's Square. Once the site of the Shanghai Race Club – in its day the lead race club in Asia – the park was created in 1952 and comprises beautiful gardens and walkways, a fun-fair for kids, the original Shanghai Race Club building (dating from 1933) plus the lauded Shanghai Museum, Grand Theatre and excellent Urban Planning Museum. If the latter sounds stodgy, think again – it's one of the city's most compelling museums. People's Park can be reached by the Metro stop at People's Square, via Lines 1, 2 and 8. On weekends, to the left of the Number 9 Metro exit, there's a fascinating matchmaker's market, where parents come to find suitable dating partners for their children.

People's Park

LU XUN PARK 鲁迅公园

This glorious park, a little north of Suzhou Creek, is where locals congregate to sing opera in groups, play Chinese instruments, dance, walk backwards, stand upside down and indulge in all manner of weird and wonderful forms of exercise. Old guys hoist their caged birds onto tree branches and happy warbling fills the air. You'll also see practitioners of *dì shū* (地书), who artfully stroke calligraphy onto concrete using a large brush moistened with water – the results are ethereal, eventually evaporating into thin air. The Ti Li Ming Tea House inside the park is a good place to chill, local style, with a simple canteen next door for noodles, dumplings and the like.

Lu Xun Park

Hongkou

WALK THE PORK OFF

HONGKOU 虹口区

While you're in the vicinity of Lu Xun Park, why not spend the whole day in Hongkou, the city's untouristed north? You'll discover remnants of the Jewish ghetto in the Tilanqiao district (无国籍难民限定地区, 提篮桥街道), great swathes of historic apartment buildings, fantastic street life, tucked away parks and the occasional temple. Snack along Jiangxi North Road, admittedly a little tatty but filled with excellent street-eats, and wander the history-filled lanes around the Ohel Moishe Synagogue. To make the most of it, book an informative tour at www.viator.com. Or simply tramp up Hongkou's main drag, Sichuan North Road, diving off into interesting side streets as the mood strikes.

Lu Xun Park

Jing'an Sculpture Park

Century Avenue

Residential Hongkou

Jing'an Sculpture Park

Jing'an Sculpture Park

WALK THE PORK OFF

FUXING PARK 复兴公园

Sited near all the buzz and retail madness of Huaihai Road, serene Fuxing Park was a private garden during the Ming Dynasty. The French took hold of it in 1909, adding Gallic touches like lakes, fountains and covered pavilions. A little remains of these today, with the plane-tree shaded paths feeling particularly Parisian. Other highlights include the rose garden, a large, central "mattress" flowerbed where plantings rotate with the seasons and the Marx and Engels Sculpture Square, dominated by a massive sculpture of the pair, erected in 1985. As with all Shanghai parks, mornings are the recommended time to visit, with locals out in force exercising, singing or playing cards.

Fuxing Park

CENTURY AVENUE 世纪大道

Leave Lujiazui Metro station on Line 2 and follow your nose to the elevated walkway that takes in the imposing Jin Mao tower, Shanghai World Financial Centre, the Shanghai Tower and luxury-brand temptations like the IFC Mall. Walk the other way and it leads right near the kooky Oriental Pearl Tower that so dominates the skyline, and down to Century Park (世纪公园). At 140 hectares, this is Shanghai's largest park and it's right near the Science and Technology Museum, if such a thing floats your boat. If you don't want to use your feet to explore the park, there are tandem bicycles for hire. Beautifully landscaped, the park boasts gardens trussed up in English, Chinese and Japanese styles. There are lovely, large ponds where some doughty locals even try their luck at fishing. You can get to

Views, Century Avenue

Century Avenue

Astor House Hotel

Yu Garden

Yu Garden

The Bund

WALK THE PORK OFF

Century Park by using the Century Park Metro stop on Line 2. Entrance to the park costs 10RMB, more on national holidays.

YU GARDEN 豫园

A highly subscribed tourist draw but utterly gorgeous all the same, Yu Garden was created in 1577 and sprawls over 20,000 picture-perfect square metres. Rock up before tickets go on sale at 8.30am, be the first through the gate, sprint ahead of the pack and have this masterpiece of Ming-era garden design pretty much to yourself – for 15 minutes at least. Paths meander through six main scenic areas that variously feature idyllic fish ponds, magnificent halls, pavilions, rockeries and cloisters. After the frantic city streets, the place is a tonic. It's easily accessed via Exit 1, Yuyuan Metro station, on Line 10.

THE BUND 外滩

A 1.5km long strip along the Huangpu River, the Bund is Shanghai's most talismanic sight. Much of the grand architecture dates from the turn of last century, when Shanghai was a world financial centre. Under the communist government, post-1949, the monolithic buildings were converted to other uses and hotels (such as the lovely old Astor House, over the Waibaidu Bridge) declined. The area wasn't revitalised until the 1980s and 1990s, when a protective levee and wide promenade were built. Whatever the time of day, there's always something happening along the Bund, making it a wonderful place to stroll. Kite-fliers come out on the weekends and every evening, the spectacular lights on the Pudong side make a splashy show. *

Snapping the Bund skyscape

China isn't known for its puddings; a platter of fruit is the usual way to wind up a meal. That's not to say Shanghai doesn't have indigenous cakes and confectionaries aplenty — the Shanghainese sweet tooth is legendary and there's more than enough sucrose flying around this town to put your dental work on notice.

EIGHT TREASURE RICE
BĀ BǍO FÀN 八宝饭

Eight treasure rice is a festive dish traditional to Shanghai and surrounding areas. The evocative name comes from the various dried fruits and nuts that stud the top of this dome-shaped treat. As with many Chinese dishes, there's a legend or two attached to its origins. One tells of an imperial cook who invented it to commemorate the victory of King Wu over a despotic ruler in 1600BC – the "treasures" represent eight warriors who fought in a particularly meritorious manner. Other accounts claim it was concocted as a gift for the Dowager Empress during the Qing Dynasty. Whatever its origins, it's delectable. Big time.

Made by steaming glutinous rice enriched with lard, the pudding is stuffed with a hefty seam of red bean paste. Thick and smooth, red bean paste is a common theme in sweet cakes in Shanghai; it's made from mashed cooked adzuki beans, lard and sugar. ▷

EIGHT TREASURE RICE 八宝饭

White glutinous rice is commonly used, although more and more places are toying with black rice, or a mixture of both black and white.

Why eight treasures? Eight (bā, 八) is an auspicious number in China as it sounds like the first part of fācái, (发财), the word for 'make a fortune'.

The decorative treasure trimmings vary, but osmanthus flowers, walnuts, red dates, lotus seeds, sultanas, dried apricots and dried longan are common.

Eight treasure rice pops up on some restaurant menus – but not by any means all – and is also available from traditional cake shops. ✱

CAKE SHOPPING
Buy all manner of local-style cakes such as this one, chì dòu gāo or "red bean cake" (赤豆糕), from the tempting, chock-full window of **Shen Da Cheng** (沈大成 南京东路店), 636 Nanjing East Road Huangpu 黄浦区南京东路636号

QĪNGTUÁN (青团)

In early spring, people clamour for plump, green dumplings called **qīngtuán.** The colour comes from the juice of a particular grass that's only edible in spring, although artificial colouring is also common, so you can easily find them all year round. *Qīngtuán* are made by steaming glutinous rice flour dough around a filling, usually sweet bean, but there are savoury pork-filled versions as well. Associated with the Qingming (Tomb Sweeping) Festival in early April, that's when they're at their best. Find good qīngtuán at **Xinhualou** (上海杏花楼), 343 Fuzhou Road, Huangpu 黄浦区 福州路343号. They can sell more than 50,000 *qīngtuán* in a single day during spring – the lines that form for them are formidable, to say the least.

WHERE TO EAT

SHUN FENG
(顺风大酒店 人民广场店)
3F, Central Plaza No 227,
North Huangpi Road, Huangpu
黄浦区 黄陂北路227号
中区广场3楼
11am–2pm, 5pm–10pm daily.
A decent dining option near People's Park, serving Shanghainese and Cantonese staples (including yum cha dishes, should you crave those). Its eight treasure rice is black-rice based and you can order a large one to serve 4–6.

DE XING GUAN
(上海德兴面馆 广东路总店)
471 Guangdong Road, Huangpu
黄浦区 广东路471号
6.30am–9.30pm daily.
Go to the on-street windows and get take-out eight treasure rice (either small or large); it's not served in either the famous downstairs canteen, nor upstairs restaurant.

FU 1088 (福1088)
375 Zhenning Road, Changning
长宁区 镇宁路375号
11am–2pm, 5.30pm–11pm daily.
A grand restaurant in a restored old villa; Shanghainese standards are presented here in an ultra-finessed fashion. The eight treasure rice is particularly suave, served as it is with a side of walnut cream.

XIAN QIANG FANG
(鲜墙房 永安大饭店)
4-5F, 600 Jiujiang Road, Huangpu
黄浦区 九江路600号4-5楼
11am–2pm, 5pm–10pm daily.
Up a creaky lift, this fabulous place has an interior frozen in the 1930s; for "old Shanghai" ambience, you won't do better. Its dried persimmon eight treasure rice is as delicious as it is pretty.

Looking to do some credit card damage? Shanghai has plenty of retail pull for the food fiend – from kitchen kitsch to groovy, Sino-themed *objets* and traditional bites and drinks, the Great Haul of China beckons. Just pretend you're buying for a friend; we won't tell a soul.

HOMEWARES

Madame Mao's Dowry is a one-stop gift shop for locally designed clothing, ephemera, homewares and more. Look for stuff from **Pinyin Press**, who put locally-inspired, stylised motifs, like the ubiquitous dumpling and waving cat, to great use on tea towels and mugs, in salt and pepper shakers and these cute paperweights. 207 Fumin Road, Xuhui 徐汇区 富民路207号10am–7pm daily.

CONFECTIONERY

Burning holes in Shanghai pearly whites since 1943, these iconic, taffy-like milk sweets were once marketed with the claim that seven of them contained a cup of milk. Sugar by any other name, you'll find myriad **White Rabbit** flavours (chocolate, peanut, red bean, matcha, etc) in cute, retro packaging at the **Shanghai No 1 Food Store, Huangpu** (上海市第一食品商店) 720 Nanjing East Road, 黄浦区 南京东路720号 9.30am–10pm daily.

COASTERS

Esydragon (手绘上海原创明信片) in Tianzifang (田子坊, see page 56) brims with gifty goods. The cute-as-a-button tea pots, smartphone cases, luggage tags, soap dispensers, etc., sport funky, colourful, China-esque motifs and make great souvenirs. What food lover wouldn't adore dumpling-emblazoned key rings, for example, or these hot-pink coasters that scream "double happiness"? Unit 51, Lane 248, 210 Taikang Road, Huangpu 黄浦区 泰康路210弄 10am–8pm daily.

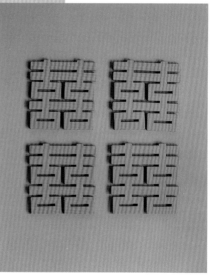

TEA

One of Shanghai's best frock and lifestyle shops, **Urban Tribe** has plenty that's gift-worthy, including these beautifully packaged teas. Buying them is as good a cover as any for a clothing splurge; the timeless lines and dreamy fabrics, inspired by rural China, sure make a statement. There are several branches but the best selection is at the flagship store in the Former French Concession.
133 Fuxing West Road, Xuhui
徐汇区 复兴西路133号
10am–10pm daily.

PORCELAIN

Ceramicist Hai Chen's **concept store** is a homewares wonderland. Handmade from kaolin clay, her porcelain goods are crafted using ancient methods and echo traditional forms. Pared-back colours and contemporary lines are her hallmarks, applied to beautiful effect on teapots, cups, plates, mugs, bowls et al.
Blue Shanghai White, Shop 17, 103 Fuzhou Road, Huangpu
黄浦区 福州路17号103室
10.30am–6.30pm daily.

COOKIES

Cookies from the famous Shanghai cookie company **Hayouwei** are perfect for giving. Get them in sweet (such as almond) or salty (such as seaweed) flavours, picking up a handful of inexpensive boxes from the mind-bending selection at the **Shanghai No 1 Food Store** (see page 123). Also available at any of the souvenir shops inside **Yuyuan Bazaar** (豫园商场)
269 Fangbang Middle Road, Huangpu
黄浦区 方浜中路269号
9am–10pm daily.

APRON

Another quirky goodie from **Madame Mao's Dowry** (see page 122), this heavy cotton apron makes playful use of the image of Lei Feng, a hero of the People's Liberation Army. Something of a cultural icon, he was once promoted by the government as a model of modesty and selflessness. Here, he seems quite at home with his wooden spoons.
207 Fumin Road, Xuhui
徐汇区 富民路207号
10am–7pm daily. *

CLEAVER

For a cook, nothing says "I love you" like a quality, well-balanced Damascus steel cleaver. **Zhang Xiao Quan** (张小泉), in business for 300 years and a famous Hangzhou-based brand, may be best known for scissors but its knives are beautiful. The flagship Shanghai shop is always packed; you'll find lovely chopsticks here too.
490 Nanjing East Road, Huangpu
黄浦区 南京东路490号
9.30am–9.30pm daily.

OVEN MITT

Gǔbù is a hardy, hand-woven calico fabric that's traditional to the Shanghai region. Sadly it's no longer made, but **Brut Cake's** owner, Nicole Teng, has stashes of the stuff and she's made it a signature of her homewares ranges. Place mats, coasters, pot holders and these cute, durable oven mitts are typical, and they all have a raw, tactile beauty.
232 Anfu Road, Xuhui
徐汇区 安福路232号
11am–7pm daily.

YELLOW WINE

A decorative bottle of local rice yellow wine (*huángjiǔ*, 黄酒) like this, or fire water (we're looking at you, *báijiǔ* 白酒) makes an excellent gift. Yellow wine, around 20% alcohol, is graded by sugar content, from dry all the way to sweet, and is best served warm. Jingfeng, a 70-year-old local brand, is tops. Find it at the **Shanghai No 1 Food Store** (上海市第一食品商店). 720 Nanjing East Road, 黄浦区 南京东路720号 9.30am–10pm daily.

ANTIQUES

Buying "antiques" in China is risky as fakes abound. There's no guarantee you'll find exactly these cute vintage soy and vinegar pourers at **Shanghai Old Street Market** (福佑路 工艺品市场), but there's always tonnes more to tempt (old bowls and plates, for example). Weekends are best; wear your Big Boy Haggle Pants and head straight to the third floor. 457 Fangbang Road, Huangpu 黄浦区 黄浦区 方浜中路457号 9am–5pm Mon–Fri, 5am–5pm Sat–Sun.

Learn some lingo

The Shanghainese have their own Chinese regional dialect, of which they're staunchly proud. But the national language, Mandarin Chinese, is in common everyday use and it's the go-to language when you want to communicate with the locals. It can seem impenetrable, not least of all because it relies on four distinct tones (high, rising, falling-rising and falling) as well as another neutral tone. So, a single word can have four entirely different meanings, depending on the tone used; it's no stretch to say that tonal subtleties are make-or-break when it comes to being understood. No pressure!

On top of this, pronunciation of both vowels and consonants can be counter-intuitive to English speakers. Novices will have slim chance of reading characters, but the key to pronunciation can be unlocked by following the *pinyin*, or Romanised, versions of the language; street signs and shop fronts often use *pinyin*. The following tips and vocabulary won't exactly guarantee fluency, but will provide basic pronunciation pointers and a few useful words and phrases.

PRONUNCIATION

"a" as in f**A**ther
"ai" as in **Ai**sle
"ao" as in h**OW**
"e" as in h**Er**
"ei" as in sl**Ei**gh
"i" as in str**EE**t
"ian" sounds like **YEN**
"ie" sounds like **YEAH**
"o" as in p**OO**r
"ou" as in c**OA**t
"u" as in c**U**te
"ui" sounds like **WAY**
"uo" sounds like **WHOA**
"yu" as in p**EA**
"c" as in ni**TS**

"ch" as in **CH**op
"q" as in **CH**eese
"sh" as in **SH**ip
"x" as in **SH**ip
"z" as in spu**DS**
"zh" as in **J**udge

BASICS

Hello (Nǐ hǎo) 你好
Goodbye
(Zàijiàn) 再见
How are you?
(Nǐ hǎo ma?) 你好吗
Thank you
(Xièxie) 谢谢
Excuse me
(Qǐngwèn) 请问

yes(shì) 是
no (búshì) 不是
please (qǐng) 请
You're welcome!
(Bú kèqì!) 不客气!
What is your name?
(Nǐ jiào shénme míngzi?)
你叫什么名字?
I don't understand
(Wǒ bù míngbái)
我不明白
Do you speak English?
(Nǐ huì shuō yīngyǔ ma?)
你会说英语吗
Can you speak slowly, please?

(Nǐ kěyǐ shuō màn yīdiǎn, qǐng?)
你可以说慢一点吗？

Do you have ....?
(Nǐ yǒu méiyǒu ...?)
你 有 没 有 ...?

How much does it cost? (Tā yào duōshǎo qián?) 它要多少钱?

Where is...?
(Zài nǎlǐ?) 在哪里...?

bathroom (cèsuǒ) 厕所
bank (yínháng) 银行
restaurant (cāntīng) 餐厅
hotel (fàndiàn) 饭店
male (nán) 男
women (nǚ) 女
entrance (rùkǒu) 入口
exit (chūkǒu) 出口
open (dǎkāi) 打开
closed (guānmén) 关门

AT THE RESTAURANT

breakfast (zǎocān) 早餐
lunch (wǔcān) 午餐
dinner (wǎncān) 晚餐
Can you recommend anything? (Yǒu shén me kě yǐ tuī jiàn de mā) 有什么可以推荐的吗？

What's the most popular dish here? (Zhè lǐ zuì huǒ de cài shì shén me?) 这里最火的菜是什么？

signature dish (zhāo pái cài) 招牌菜
I'd like to order... (Diǎn cài...) 点菜...
One serving of this

(pointing to menu)
(Zhè gè, yī fèn)
这个，一份

I am a vegetarian
(Wǒ shì sù) 我吃素

Please bring me a menu (bāng máng ná gè càidān)
帮忙拿个菜单

I would like...
(Wò xiǎngyào...)
我想要...

I would like a glass of water please
(Qǐng gěi wǒ yī bēi shuǐ)
请给我一杯水

Do you have an English menu?
(Néng gěi wǒ yīngwén càidān ma?)
能给我英文菜单吗？

I don't eat...
(Wǒ bù chī...)
我不吃...

I don't eat nuts
(Wǒ bù chī jiānguǒ)
我不吃坚果

I am allergic to gluten
(Wǒ duì miànjīn guòmǐn)
我对面筋过敏

That was delicious
(Zhège hào chī)
这个好吃

Cheers! (Gānbēi!) 干杯

The bill, please
(Máfan mǎidān)
麻烦买单

Can I use a credit card?
(Shuā kǎ kě yǐ mā?)
刷卡可以吗？

I would like to pay,

please
(Wǒ xiǎng mǎidān)
我想买单

We will pay together
(Wǒmen yīqǐ fù qián)
我们一起付钱

We will pay separately
(Wǒmen fēnkāi jiézhàng)
我们分开结账

A FEW FOOD AND DRINK WORDS

beer (píjiǔ) 啤酒
tea (chá) 茶
red wine (hóngpútáojiǔ) 红葡萄酒
white wine (báipútáojiǔ) 白葡萄酒
local wine (dāngdì de pútáojiǔ) 当地的葡萄酒
restaurant (cān tīng) 餐廳
waiter/waitress (fú wù shēng) 服务生
spoon (tāng chí) 湯匙
fork (chā zi) 叉子
knife (dāo zi) 刀子
chopsticks (kuài zi) 筷子
bowl (wǎn) 碗
glass (bēizi) 杯子
bottle (píngzi) 瓶子
cold (lěng) 冷
bill (jiézhàng) 结账
soy sauce (jiàngyóu) 酱油
vinegar (cù) 醋
ginger (shēngjiāng) 生姜
chilli (làjiāo) 辣椒
menu (cài dān) 菜單 ▷

one portion (yí fèn)
一份

water (shuǐ) 水

boiled water (kāishuǐ)
开水

mineral water
(kuàngquánshuǐ) 矿泉水

soup (tāng) 汤

vegetables (shūcài)
蔬菜

rice (mǐfàn) 米饭

meat (ròu) 肉

noodles (miàntiáo)
面条

pork (zhūròu) 猪肉

chicken (jīròu) 鸡肉

beef (niúròu) 牛肉

fish (yú) 鱼

peanuts (huāshēng)
花生

eggs (dàn) 蛋

spicy (là) 辣

NUMBERS

0 (líng) 0
1 (yī) 一
2 (èr/liǎng*) 二/两
3 (sān) 三
4 (sì) 四
5 (wǔ) 五
6 (liù) 六
7 (qī) 七
8 (bā) 八
9 (jiǔ) 九
10 (shí) 十
11 (shíyī) 十一
12 (shíèr) 十二
13 (shísān) 十三
14 (shísì) 十四
15 (shíwǔ) 十五
16 (shíliù) 十六

17 (shíqī) 十七
18 (shíbā) 十八
19 (shíjiǔ) 十九
20 (èrshí) 二十
30 (sānshí) 三十
40 (sìshí) 四十
50 (wǔshí) 五十
60 (liùshí) 六十
70 (qīshí) 七十
80 (bāshí) 八十
90 (jiǔshí) 九十
100 (yìbǎi) 一百
1000 (yīqiān) 一千
* **liǎng** 两 [is used for 2
when counting people
and things.

DIRECTIONS AND TRANSPORT

subway station
(dìtiězhàn) 地铁站

taxi (chūzū chē)
出租车

airport (jīchǎng)
机场

What is the address?
(Tā dì dìzhǐ zài nǎlǐ?)
它的地址在哪里?

Is it far to walk?
(Yào zǒu hěn yuǎn ma?)
要走很远吗?

in front of

(zài qiánmiàn) 在前面

opposite (duìmiàn)
对面

next to (pángbiān de)
旁边的

on the corner
(zài jiǎoluò) 在角落

**on the other side of
the street**
(zài jiēdào de lìng yìbiān)
街道的另一边

Where is...?
(Zài nǎlǐ...?) 在哪里...?

I am lost (Wǒ mílùle)
我迷路了

**Can you write the
address, please?**
(Kěyǐ máfan nǐ xiě xià
dìzhǐ ma?)
可以麻烦你写下地址
吗?

**Can you show me on
the map?**
(Nǐ néng zài dìtú shàng
zhǐ gěi wǒ kàn ma?)
你能在地图上指给我
看吗

turn left (zuǒ zhuǎn)
左转

turn right (yòu zhuǎn)
右转

walk straight ahead
(zhí zǒu) 直走 *

GOOD TO KNOW

When navigating your way around Shanghai streets,
bear in mind that street names often incorporate:
east (dōng 东), **west** (xi 西), **north** (běi 北),
south (nán 南) **middle** (zhōng 中. The word for
road is lù 路 while **street** is jiē 街.

THE CHARACTER FOR
'SAUCE' (*jiàng* 酱) PAINTED
ON A SHANGHAI WALL

Notes

Shanghai In 12 Dishes
Published by RedPorkPress
P.O. Box 10003, Dominion Road, Auckland, 1446 New Zealand
www.redporkpress.com

 www.facebook.com/redporkpress
 www.instagram.com/redporkpress
 www.twitter.com/redporkpress

Publishing executive: Antony Suvalko
Editorial director: Leanne Kitchen
Art direction and design: Anne Barton
Copy editor: Karen Lateo
Language consultant: Sarah Wong
Words and photography: ©RedPorkPress

While RedPorkPress has taken all reasonable care in the making of this book,
we make no warranty about the accuracy or completeness of its content and,
to the maximum extent permitted, disclaim any liability arising from its use.
Travellers are advised to check for updates prior to travel.

First edition – April 2017

ISBN 9780473379087

Printed in China

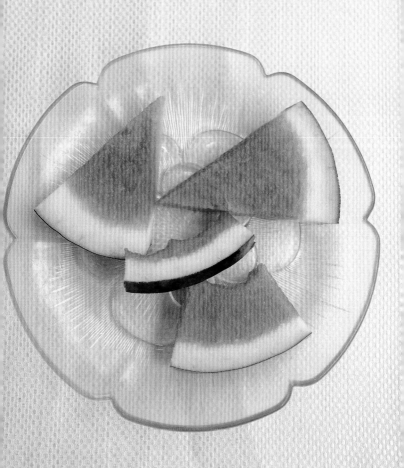

FOOD AND BREAKFAST STREETS

1. Nanyan/Xikang Road
2. Zhejiang Middle Road
3. Zhejiang South Road
4. Ningbo Road
5. Zhapu Road
6. Yunnan South Road
7. Wulumuqi Road

M50 ◆

Shangh
Railwo
Station

Tianmu West Road

Changshou Road

Jade
Buddha
Temple

23

Jiangning Road

Shimen No 2 Road

Kangding Road

JING'AN

Jing'an Sculpture Park

Beijing West Road

32 Jing'an
    Temple

33 1 35

Nanjing West Road

36

38

Weihai Road

TO SUZHOU

TO HONGQUAO
AIRPORT

TIANSHAN
TEA CITY

17 18

Yan'an Middle Road

Yan'an West Road

Julu Road

Shimen No 1 Road

1 30

Anfu Road

Changshu Road

Changle Road

20 27

6

16 3 58

7

Huaihai Middle Road

Rujin No 1 Road

Fuxing Middle Road

31

Fuxing Park ◆

Chongqing So

4 41

69

XUHUI

12 50

43

Rujin No 2 Road

Tianzifang ◆

26

10

TO QIBAO

7

Luban Road

136